Zero Trust Security for Beginners

A no-fluff guide to implementing Zero Trust architecture using NIST.

Taimur Ijlal

About this book

This edition was published in **May 2023**

I have tried to keep it as up to date as possible, but Zero Trust is an ever-evolving discipline, and I will regularly update this book over time.

Copyright © 2023 Taimur Ijlal

All rights reserved.

DEDICATION

This book is dedicated to my wife and parents. My wife, who regularly pushes me to take on new challenges and risks to better myself. My parents raised me to be the person I am today and never let me feel that I could not achieve what I set my mind to.

Thanks to everyone who watches my YouTube Channel, "Cloud Security Guy," and I appreciate all the comments/feedback I receive.

Lastly, **THANK YOU** for purchasing this book, and I hope it helps increase your practical understanding of Zero Trust.

Taimur Ijlal

CONTENTS

Table of Contents

1 - Introduction 2
    Why should I read this book? 4
    Do you already have a course on this? 6
    Did you write this book using ChatGPT? 7

2 – The Need for Zero Trust 8
    So, what exactly is Zero Trust? 11
    Isn't all of this already being done? 13
    What are Zero Trust principles? 15
    Summing it all up 16

3 – A brief history of Zero Trust 18
    No more Chewy Centers 18
    Google BeyondCorp 19
    NIST SP 800-207 Published 21
    Executive Order (EO) 14028 22
    Chapter Summary 23

4 – A look at Zero Trust principles 25
    Zero Trust Foundational Principles 25
        1 - Never Trust; always Verify 26
        2 - Enforce Least privilege 26
        3 - Enforce microsegmentation 27
        4 - Continuous monitoring and analytics 29
        5 - Apply trust dynamically using intelligent policies 30

Zero Trust Principles as per NIST 32

Summing it all up 36

4 – Understanding the NIST Zero Trust standard 37

Zero Trust architecture as per NIST 38
    1 - The Control Plane and Data Plane 38
    2 - The Subject and the resource 39
    3 - The Policy Decision Point (PDP) 39
    4 - The Policy Enforcement Point (PEP) 40
    5 - Importance of the PDP and PEP 41
    6 - Contextual Data Sources 42

Summing it all up 45

5 – Zero Trust variations and models 47

A - NIST architecture approaches 48
    1 - Enhanced Identity Governance 48
    2 - Micro-Segmentation 48
    3 - Network Infrastructure & Software-Defined Perimeters 49
    Which is the best approach? 49

B - NIST deployed variations 50
    1 - Device Agent/Gateway-Based 50
    2 - Enclave-Based 51
    3 - Resource Portal 51
    4 - Device Application Sandboxing 52

C - Zero Trust scenarios 53
    1 - Enterprise with Satellite Facilities 54
    2 - Multi-Cloud/Cloud-to-Cloud Enterprise 54
    3 - Contracted Services/Nonemployee Access 55
    4 - Collaboration across Enterprise Boundaries 55
    5 - Enterprise with Public/Customer-Facing Services 55

D - Zero Trust Threats 56
    1 - Bypass the decision process 56
    2 - Make the PDP or PEP unavailable 57
    3 - Stolen credentials 58

  4 - Lack of visibility 59
  5 - Storage of sensitive information 59

 Chapter Summary 61

6 – A Zero Trust case study 63

 Company ABC 63
  Step 1 - Assessing the architecture. 66
  Step 2 - Deciding upon the PDP 68
  Step 3 - Deciding upon the PEP 69
  Step 4 - What about microsegmentation 71
  Step 5 - The Cloud environment 73
  Step 6 - Presenting to the CISO for feedback. 74

 Your Zero Trust roadmap 77
  Phase 1 - Putting a foundation 77
  Phase 2 - Filling in the gaps 78

 Summing it all up 79

7 – How to start a Zero Trust Project 81

 1 - Get management buy in 82

 2 - Understand and map the environment 84

 3 - Introduce control mechanisms 85

 4 - Implement Zero Trust model 87

 5 - Maintain and improve the model 88

 Chapter Summary 90

8 – Zero Trust Challenges 93

 Challenges to implementing ZTA. 93

 Lack of Zero Trust support 94
  Enclave-Based deployment model 95
  Zero Trust proxy 96

9 – Where to go from here 101

Keep in touch. **102**

Training and Courses **102**

Feedback time **102**

ABOUT THE AUTHOR

Taimur Ijlal is a multi-award-winning information security leader with over two decades of international experience in cyber-security and IT risk management in the fin-tech industry. For his contributions to the industry, he won a few awards here and there, such as CISO of the Year, CISO Top 30, CISO Top 50, and Most Outstanding Security Team.

He served as the Head of Information Security for several major companies, but his real passion is teaching and writing about cyber-security topics. He lives in the UK, where he moved with his family in 2021.

Taimur regularly writes on Medium and has a YouTube channel, "Cloud Security Guy," on which he posts about Cloud Security, Artificial Intelligence, and general cyber-security career advice.

He has also launched several Cyber-Security and Artificial Intelligence courses and can be contacted on his LinkedIn profile for any consulting opportunities.

1 - Introduction

Zero Trust is one of the most exciting concepts I have ever worked on or written on in my two-decades-long career in Cybersecurity.

It is also one of the most misunderstood.

When I started researching **Zero Trust Architecture** and trying to implement it a few years back, I faced the following challenges:

- Most of the material on Zero Trust architecture is very high-level and not specific enough to implement.
- There is not enough practical advice about implementing Zero Trust principles.
- The detailed stuff on Zero Trust is very vendor-driven and focused on products instead of explaining the concept, i.e., *buy our XYZ product and get Zero Trust certified today!*

I had to sift through much fluff to finally get a thorough practical understanding of Zero Trust, which I also turned into a course (more on that later).

Once that course was launched and became one of the highest-rated courses on Udemy, I realized that I had quite a lot of material left over that did not make it into the system. Enough to write a book, and here we are.

My reasons for writing this book are simple. This book **will**:

- Tell you about the fundamental principles and components of Zero Trust architecture.
- Inform you about the importance of Zero Trust in modern security and its benefits and challenges.
- Teach core components such as Policy Decision Point (PDP), Policy Enforcement Point (PEP), Zero Trust proxies, etc.
- Inform you about the NIST SP 800-207 guidelines for implementing a Zero Trust architecture.
- Teach you about assessing and improving Zero Trust maturity within an organization.

As the book cover says, this is a "no-fluff" handbook, so I have tried to remove any padding and ensure you get value quickly.

I have also provided practical scenarios and case studies so you get actionable advice on implementing Zero Trust within your environment.

There are also a few things this book does not do.

For example, this book does not:

- Tell you about a specific technology or Zero Trust product. I will not promote or recommend any solution, as that is not the point of this book.

- Give you a shortcut to implementing Zero Trust. Making your environment compliant with Zero Trust principles is a huge undertaking; each company uses and implements technology differently. *If you want to know how to implement Zero Trust in 24 hours, this is not the book.*

Why should I read this book?

Implementing and improving a cybersecurity architecture is a difficult job. You need to understand how your environment works, the key areas to focus on, AND where the weak points are.

Today's environments are a mesh of on-prem servers, cloud applications, serverless functions, microservices, and on and on. On top of that, you have remote workers and partners wanting to access the environment and do their job.

Most companies go too far in one direction; they either put in too many controls making life hell for employees, or leave the environments too open, making life easy for cybercriminals.

We need a new security model to accommodate modern networks; this is where Zero Trust Architecture or ZTA comes in.

ZTA brings a new modern approach to designing your environments and enforces certain principles that can accommodate modern technologies while maintaining the security posture of your network and applications. It assumes that the network is already compromised OR will likely get compromised, limiting network access to the bare minimum.

Is it a perfect concept? NO

Is it foolproof? NO

Is it necessary for today's networks? YES,

There is a reason that Gartner estimates that *".. by 2025, at least 70% of new remote access deployments will be served predominantly by ZTNA as opposed to VPN services, up from less than 10% at the end of 2021."*

There is also a reason that the Biden Administration made Zero Trust a crucial part of its Executive Order for improving the nation's cybersecurity, stating that:

*"The Federal Government must adopt security best practices; advance toward **Zero Trust Architecture**; accelerate movement to secure cloud services, including Software as a Service (SaaS), Infrastructure as a Service (IaaS), and Platform as a Service (PaaS); centralize and streamline access to cybersecurity data to drive analytics for identifying and managing cybersecurity risks; and invest in both technology and personnel to match these modernization goals."*

To (mis)quote Gordon Gekko from the movie 'Wall Street' ... **"Zero Trust works."**

Provided you implement it correctly, the result is a safer and more secure network where you can dynamically enforce policies based on different contexts.

One key point is that the term "Zero Trust" might be a bit misleading as in a ZTA environment, you have Zero "**implicit**" Trust, i.e., no one is trusted right off the bat just because they are sitting within the network or coming from a corporate device. Instead, trust is earned in a ZTA architecture based on various policies you define and can be revoked if the model feels something has changed within the user's behavior or profile.

This makes ZTA a living, breathing security model instead of the static "*allow traffic from X IP address*" way of doing things.

Do you already have a course on this?

The answer is **YES,** and I do very much have a course on this which you can access below:

https://www.udemy.com/course/zero-trust-masterclass-from-beginner-to-mastery/

However, like my other book on Artificial Intelligence Cybersecurity and Governance, this book complements the course and does not replace it. There will be overlap in the topics that are taught, but some people prefer reading books while some like to listen and follow along, so it depends on which style of learning you like (or you can do both and get the best of both worlds)

Did you write this book using ChatGPT?

The answer to that is NO. I love ChatGPT, and I know many people are doing very cool stuff with it. But no ... this book results from my strenuous efforts and hours sitting before my laptop.

I do plan to write a book on ChatGPT soon, so let's see how that goes.

Feedback is always appreciated.

Lastly, please leave a review and let me know what you liked and where you think it can be improved. I always appreciate feedback, whether it is positive or negative, as that will help me improve as a writer and make better material.

It just takes a minute and will be very helpful !

2 – The Need for Zero Trust

Before we dive deep into Zero trust as a concept, let us first understand the need for Zero Trust.

Why do we need a new buzzword to add to the thousands of other buzzwords already in the cybersecurity industry?

To appreciate Zero Trust, let us take a walk down memory lane. In the good old days, we did not need to worry about Zero Trust as we had the perimeter approach. It consisted of a strong network perimeter defined by Firewalls, Intrusion Prevention / Detection Systems (IDS / IPS), and all sorts of monitoring.

In a nutshell, your network architecture defines your security posture.

The perimeter model gets much flak as being outdated and insecure, but it remains the most popular model by far and is still deployed in thousands of networks worldwide.

GOOD OLD DAYS

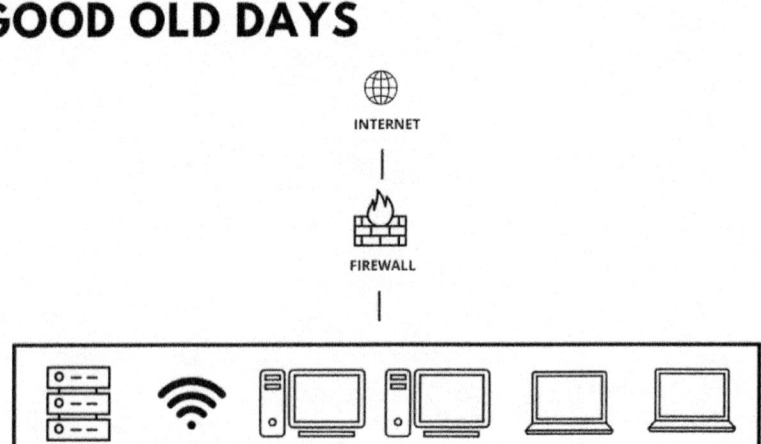

However, despite all the good it has done, it is evident that the perimeter model is too outdated by today's standards. Modern-day threats are easily able to bypass the network perimeter and move undetected once they are inside.

On top of that, we have enterprise trends such as cloud computing, bring your device (BYOD), remote working partners, etc., all of which exist outside your network boundary and on which it might not be possible to enforce your controls.

NEED FOR ZERO TRUST

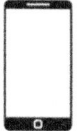    

You might be thinking, wait! You are aware of this and have controls within the perimeter like hardening, network segmentation, monitoring, anti-malware controls, etc... Still, the point here is that the *network architecture ceases to be a security control in and of itself.*

Within your network, you might have segmented the critical resources into a separate network segment which is as per best practices. However, pathways and firewall exceptions are always present for business users, system administrators, etc., that allow network traffic to pass through.

Often, these are simple firewall rules stating, *"allow x traffic from y source,"* with a comment on why this exception was added. Over time these can pile up with an annual or quarterly cleanup happening in companies that are particular about it.

Once you look carefully at this model, you can see the problems here. If this user is compromised via malware or social engineering, then attackers have a direct pathway to the critical resources.

Firewalls will not help as they usually enforce decisions based on the source and destination of the request coming through.

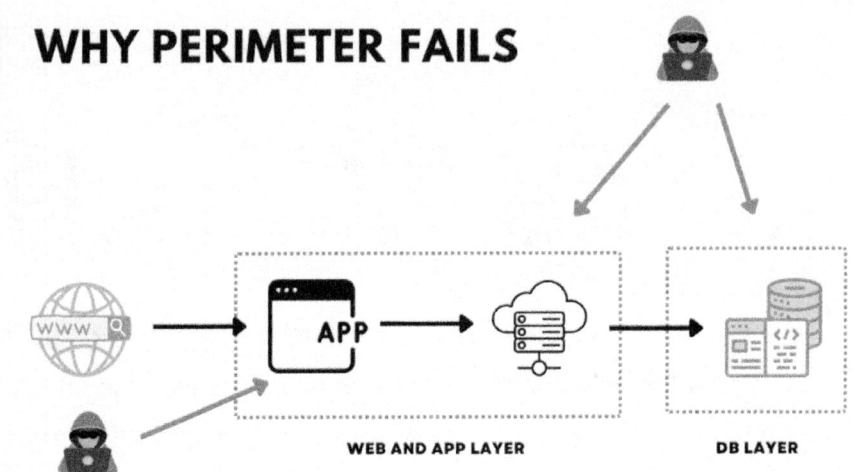

One solution would be to implement security products based on AI and Machine Learning that baseline user activity and identify deviations which is all good.

Another way is to re-evaluate this entire model and see if there is another way of granting access and evaluating user posture.

This is where Zero Trust comes in.

So, what exactly is Zero Trust?

Zero Trust, in its essence, is a framework for designing a secure architecture for today's modern enterprises. It considers modern-day challenges such as the ones we mentioned, like remote working, cloud environment, BYOD, etc., unlike the traditional "*bad guys out, good guys in*" approach.

Despite what many people think, the perimeter does not go away entirely in a Zero Trust Architecture. Instead, its role as the primary enforcement mechanism is changed. Location ceases to be the primary criterion for trusting someone and allowing them access.

Zero Trust does this by focusing on resources like users, services, workflows, and **WHAT** they are doing instead of **WHERE** they are coming from.

For a Zero Trust Architecture, the network can be on-prem, cloud-based, hybrid, etc., with requests from corporate, personal, or partner locations. It is all the same!

So, it is a design philosophy based on foundational principles and not a commercial product or certification. Along with a secure architecture, it also provides increased visibility and controls into an environment allowing cybersecurity teams to detect and respond to threats with increased speed.

There are numerous ways to implement Zero Trust, which is one of the beauties of this approach. It is also able to deal with modern challenges such as the following:

- **Remote Working**: Zero Trust removes the location from the equation and provides a security model to deal with remote or distributed teams and protect resources using intelligent policy decisions.
- **Cloud environments**: Same as remote work, by taking the

network perimeter out of the question, Zero Trust can quickly adapt to a cloud environment and protect data and applications that are not present on-prem.
- **BYOD**: Properly implemented, Zero Trust can eliminate the need for VPNs and enforce policies based on the nature of the request, device posture, risk score, etc.

Zero Trust can do all this by implementing critical controls, such as context-aware policies that consider the request's entire context, i.e., the user location, role, risk score, device posture, etc., instead of just the source and the destination.

Additionally, it enforces network-level least privilege by implementing **microsegmentation** in which the network is divided into smaller software-based segments that allow granular access controls and policies. This stops attackers from moving from one resource to another later within the same part.

NOTE: If this sounds like much gibberish, then don't worry, as we will look at all of these in detail in the coming chapters

Isn't all of this already being done?

I admit that I was highly skeptical when I first read about Zero Trust. It sounded like much technobabble about stuff already being done!

We already have policies, least privilege, segmentation, and all the other stuff Zero Trust discusses.

But this is where I needed clarification on what Zero Trust is all about.

Zero Trust does not tell you to implement something dramatically new that no one has ever heard about. It guides how to structure your network using these tools so that it can adapt and manage the ever-evolving threat landscape.

Once you understand and accept this, Zero Trust becomes much simpler to understand AND implement.

You have two choices:

1. **CHOICE 1:** Implement many disconnected solutions and mature them over time using your subjective criteria. Keep in mind that reducing risk in modern networks is not just a matter of replacing technology but the mindset.
2. **CHOICE 2**: Implement a Zero Trust Architecture in which all these solutions fall under an overarching security model defined by security best practices. You know where you stand and how you need to improve.

You can see why 2 is the logical way to go and how it can help provide you with a complete security roadmap for maturity.

Many companies might already have Zero Trust principles implemented within their enterprise and can start their official journeys with just a few tweaks here and there. Others might need time, effort, and MONEY to get it going. Regardless of where you start, remember that Zero Trust is a multi-year project that takes time and effort to mature.

What are Zero Trust principles?

Zero trust consists of a set of principles that are constantly evolving and being updated. The goal, however, is always the same; move security away from the perimeter and towards the user, assets, and resources within the network.

If we were to summarize the key ones, then they would be:

- **Never trust; always verify.**
- **Assume the network is already compromised and external/internal threats are present.**
- **Network locality is not sufficient for deciding trust in a network.**
- **Every device, user, and network flow is authenticated and authorized.**
- **Policies must be dynamic and calculated from as many data sources as possible.**

There might be many other principles, but these can be considered foundational ones that we will examine in more detail. When companies start their Zero Trust journeys, they usually assess where they stand about these principles and then incrementally implement them over time.

It is common for most companies to exist in a hybrid environment where both traditional and zero-trust architectures are present and slowly mature over time.

Summing it all up

I hope this gave you a good idea of why Zero Trust is important and how it can help mature your cybersecurity architecture. As I said, zero Trust is a journey that matures over time and not something you implement and forget about.

In the next chapter, we will look at the history of Zero Trust and how it has grown in importance over time.

3 – A brief history of Zero Trust

Zero Trust has become extremely popular but is not a recently introduced concept. Its core ideas, such as following least privilege, segmentation, and continuous monitoring, have all existed in cybersecurity long before.

This chapter will look at how this concept has evolved over the years, from its humble beginnings in 2010 to being mentioned as one of the critical principles of U.S. national security!

No more Chewy Centers

In 2010, John Kindervag introduced the Zero Trust model, highlighting that traditional cybersecurity models relying on firewalls and a network perimeter were insufficient.

The perimeter was dissolving quickly as trends like cloud computing, remote working, and BYOD rose. The Zero Trust model was proposed as a solution that assumed that all users, devices, and network traffic were untrusted until they could prove themselves.

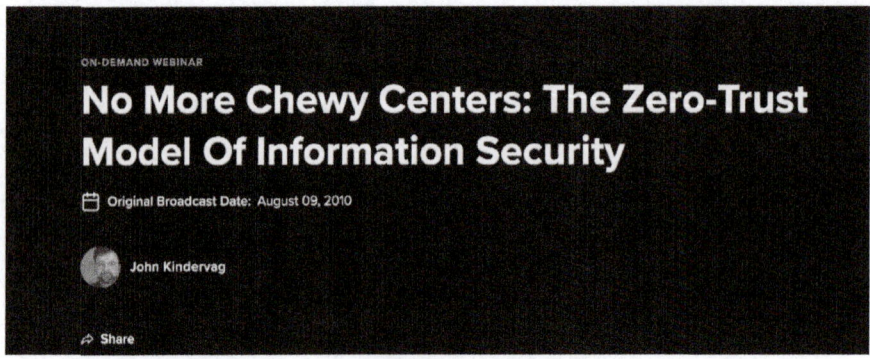

This is where Zero Trust started as a concept. Over the years, it has become increasingly popular, with its principles finding their way into many best practice frameworks. As technology has evolved and cloud computing and remote work have become more popular, the relevance of Zero Trust has grown exponentially.

It has also matured as a concept as its implementations have increased despite the foundational principles remaining the same. Vendors have also jumped on the bandwagon with new technologies and products released that are Zero Trust compatible.

Google BeyondCorp

Another significant milestone in the history of Zero Trust would be Google BeyondCorp. This project was Google's internal implementation of Zero Trust principles with their long-term vision of removing their network boundary entirely, i.e., decoupling the network perimeter from security decisions.

As they stated:

"As companies adopt mobile and cloud technologies, the perimeter is becoming increasingly difficult to enforce. Google is taking a different approach to network security. We are removing the requirement for a privileged intranet and moving our corporate applications to the Internet."

The primary goal of BeyondTrust was to securely enable Google employees to access their resources without relying on VPNs or traditional network segmentation. Instead, Zero Trust principles were used to assess user risk, device posture, risk score, etc., before granting access. Although initially an internal Google project only, the tech giant decided to share their approach with the world via a series of whitepapers detailing their implementation.

Google also created the BeyondTrust Alliance which is a group of partners that share its Zero Trust vision in a plan to "democratize" this security model.

This paved the way for widespread implementation within the industry and influenced a lot of companies to start their zero-trust journeys. Google has gone on to expand this BeyondTrust model via other whitepapers, which has become a benchmark within the industry of what Zero Trust can do.

NIST SP 800-207 Published

In August 2020, the National Institute of Standards and Technology (NIST) released SP 800-207, "*Zero Trust Architecture*," which provides best practices and guidelines on designing and implementing a Zero Trust architecture.

NIST is well known within the industry for releasing best practice documents. This standard details Zero Trust, its principles, key components, and how to implement it within an organization. It also highlights key features, such as Policy Decision Points and Policy Enforcement Engines, essential in a true Zero Trust Architecture.

The NIST document is widely used within the industry as a de facto standard for the following reasons:

- It details cloud and hybrid environments and how to model Zero Trust in such environments. It is vendor and technology neutral allowing it to be used by any company.
- The document has undergone heavy scrutiny and feedback from various experts within the industry, as with most NIST standards.
- It provides a high-level roadmap for how companies can implement a ZTA within their environment.

Executive Order (EO) 14028

Another significant milestone for Zero Trust came from Executive Order (EO) 14028 issued by U.S. President Joe Biden in May 2021. After sophisticated, high-profile cyber-attacks such as SolarWinds in 2020 and the Colonial Pipeline attack in 2021, there was an urgent need to set down a tone for improving cybersecurity at a national level.

One of the critical mandates of the order is for the U.S. Federal Agencies to take steps towards Zero Trust implementation via the NIST 800-207 standard explicitly stating:

"(b) Within 60 days of the date of this order, the head of each agency shall:

(i) update existing agency plans to prioritize resources for adopting and using cloud technology as outlined in relevant OMB

guidance.

(ii) develop a plan to implement Zero Trust Architecture, which shall incorporate, as appropriate, the migration steps that the National Institute of Standards and Technology (NIST) within the Department of Commerce has outlined in standards and guidance, describe any such actions that have already been completed, identify activities that will have the most immediate security impact, and include a schedule to implement them; and."

As can be imagined, this is a significant endorsement for Zero Trust, with the federal government being a major stakeholder in the cybersecurity industry. Adopting Zero Trust at the government level will also ripple effect on the private sector as numerous companies look to the federal level for guidance on best practices.

Chapter Summary

I hope this gave you a good idea of how Zero Trust has evolved as a concept and how its importance has increased in recent years. Over time, Zero Trust has matured into a comprehensive security model covering a broad range of technologies and principles.

As cyber threats evolve, Zero Trust will continue to play an essential role in the industry, especially with the ongoing support from governments and tech leaders.

4 – A look at Zero Trust principles

Now that we have discussed Zero Trust and its history let's take a more in-depth look at Zero Trust principles. You can implement any technology or certifications you want, but you must remember these principles to implement a Zero Trust architecture. These principles are what define this concept, after all.

Zero Trust Foundational Principles

An important point to remember when we start is that there is no fixed number of Zero Trust principles. These principles serve as the foundation for implementing a Zero Trust security strategy. They can be adapted and expanded upon to fit an organization's unique needs, considering the data type, applications, and systems that must be protected.

So do not get confused if the wording or phrasing changes from document to document, such as in the NIST standard, as different organizations interpret them differently. Still, the following are universally considered to be the core principles.

1 - Never Trust; always Verify

The most well-known principle from which all the others follow is **"Never trust, always verify."** This principle asserts that network location is not sufficient to prove an implicit trust of a user, device, or service. Operate under the mindset that the requesting entity compromised so that intelligent security measures can be applied. Every request must be explicitly authenticated regardless of where it comes from.

NORMAL APPROACH VS ZERO TRUST

TRUST BUT VERIFY   NEVER TRUST ALWAYS VERIFY

2 - Enforce Least privilege

The "enforce least privilege" principle states that user and system access must be limited to the minimum level required for accomplishing their tasks. You might be scratching your head and thinking cybersecurity teams have been doing this for years.

While this may be true, the network is a critical aspect that gets missed when applying least privilege.

Too often, applications in a shared network subnet can talk to each other without needing the same, thus violating the principle of least privilege and increasing the "blast radius" of an attack.

This leads us to the following principle of micro-segmentation.

3 - Enforce microsegmentation

As mentioned, network segmentation does not fully apply the least privilege principle, and traffic within network subnets is not restricted. Typically network security devices like firewalls have visibility into and inspect "**north-south**" traffic that crosses the perimeter. They are blind to "**east-wes**t" traffic and apply implicit trust, which goes against our first zero trust principle.

An attacker could potentially abuse this blind spot to move between workloads without any hindrance laterally.

NEED FOR MICROSEGMENTATION

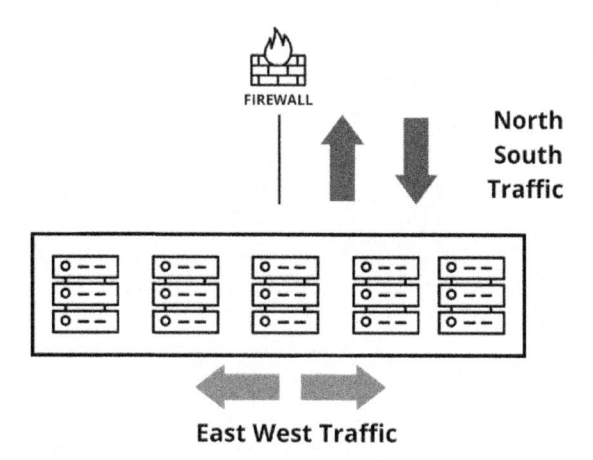

Microsegmentation is a relatively new concept in which a network is further broken down into smaller, isolated segments, making lateral movement impossible. By setting these secure zones, microsegmentation lays down a secure network defined per Zero Trust architecture in which only explicitly trusted traffic is allowed.

NEED FOR MICROSEGMENTATION

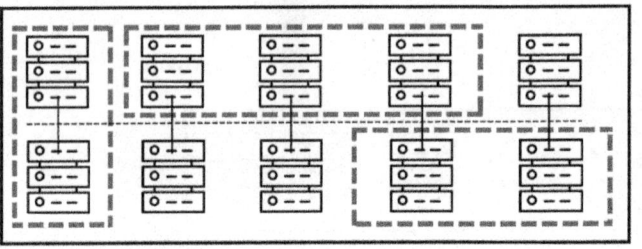

Sensitive subnet WITH microsegmentation

Keep in mind that microsegmentation compliments but does not replace traditional network firewalls. Both north-south and east-west traffic inspection is required for a secure network architecture to be present. Microsegmentation can be deployed using software agents or native cloud services, so a complete network re-architecting is unnecessary.

4 - Continuous monitoring and analytics

Zero Trust acknowledges that the days of getting and responding to an email alert are long gone. It requires every user, device, and system to be monitored to identify potential security threats and generate a baseline of user activity. We are not talking about buying a solution that collects logs and then creating alerts that no one ever looks at but using tools like machine learning to monitor and "learn" the network intelligently.

Zero trust needs to know about user behavior over a historical period, the device posture, network traffic, previous risk scores, etc. A **Security information and event management (SIEM)** solution can provide some of this information. It is one of the essential components of a Zero Trust architecture, but it is not the only one. Other equally important sources include the SSO identity provider, internal and external Threat intelligence feeds, certificate authorities, etc.

This monitoring is what is used in Zero Trust to decide if a user or request can be "trusted" or not, as we see in the following principle. Continuous monitoring helps to ensure that this trust always remains relevant and secure.

5 - Apply trust dynamically using intelligent policies

Continuous monitoring leads nicely into this principle which is applying trust dynamically using innovative policies. The keywords here are "*dynamically*" and "*intelligent.*"

Too often, security policies in traditional networks are extremely binary, with a go/no-go decision based on where they are coming from (IP address) or if they have been authenticated already.

HOW DO WE CALCULATE TRUST

EXPLICIT POLICY (OLD WAY)

- DENIED
- ALLOWED
- DENIED

Context is rarely (if ever!) considered, and dynamic risk is not calculated based on a real-time view of what the user has been doing recently. This is also due to having a siloed approach to security tooling, which makes it challenging to gain a comprehensive view of the security posture of the incoming request.

By contrast, the new approach of Zero Trust is to have adaptive and context-driven policies that adjust dynamically depending on various factors like user risk level, device posture, location, and threat intelligence data. Zero Trust promotes integrating sources of security data so that visibility is achieved and a unified way of assessing risk can be accomplished.

These policies can be changed in real-time as information about users and devices changes, making them a giant leap forward compared to the previous approach. A user that might have had access granted previously can find himself needing to re-authenticate, apply multi-factor authentication, or be denied access altogether due to a changed risk posture.

HOW DO WE CALCULATE TRUST

ZERO TRUST (NEW WAY)

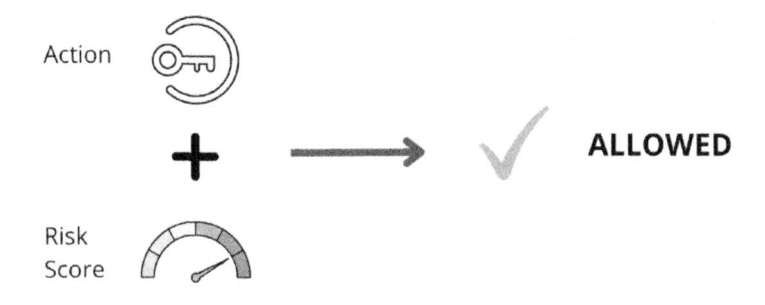

Action + Risk Score → ✓ **ALLOWED**

You can see just how much of a game changer this new approach can be, which applies trust dynamically using intelligence policies. Companies can completely change how they evaluate security posture in a Zero Trust environment. This also helps reduce the risk of malicious attackers moving within the network as access control changes depending on real-time risk levels.

Zero Trust Principles as per NIST

We discussed the importance of the NIST Special Publication "Zero Trust Architecture," or SP 800-207, released in 2020. This document provides guidelines and recommendations for implementing an authentic Zero Trust security architecture across various scenarios. It has become many companies' de facto standard for Zero Trust.

The document does not explicitly mention Zero Trust principles but refers to core tents which are the same thing. NIST makes an important point: "*These tenets are the ideal goal, though it must be acknowledged that not all principles may be fully implemented in their purest form for a given strategy.*"

Let us look at whether they align with the principles we discussed earlier.

1 - All data sources and computing services are considered resources

Most cybersecurity teams consider their internal assets, like servers and endpoints, as resources that must be protected. This worked well previously but needs to be revised for a Zero Trust mindset.

You have to take into account the following:

- Users are accessing Software as a Service (SaaS) system.
- Personal devices with access to enterprise resources
- Serverless functions that are being used by business applications.
- Any other data source or computing service with the potential to impact your environment.

Consider all of them as resources that can impact the security posture and must provide data for determining trust when access decisions are made.

2 - All communication is secured regardless of

network location

NIST stresses the same point we discussed earlier *"Network location alone does not imply trust."* The exact security requirements apply whether on the network or connecting from home. No implicit trust is granted, and visibility is restricted to only what you need access to on the web. Gone are the days of connecting from a VPN and having full access to a network.

3 - Access to individual enterprise resources is granted on a per-session basis

This tenet means that trust is an evolving and ever-changing parameter within Zero Trust. Trust is evaluated every time before a session is granted. Even if you were trusted to carry out a particular action previously, it might not be given again the next time. By restricting trust to a single session, Zero Trust ensures that a potentially compromised user or device cannot pivot or misuse this access as their risk posture changes.

4 - A dynamic policy determines access to resources

We discussed this earlier, but it bears repeating again simply due to how important this principle or tenet is. A Zero trust environment uses context-driven "signals" from all the resources and adjusts its policies accordingly. For example, a user may be given limited access, denied access, or asked to re-authenticate depending on their risk score derived from location, time, device posture, and other factors.

5 - The enterprise monitors and measures the integrity and security posture of all owned and associated assets.

If no implicit trust is present for enterprise-owned or personal assets, then continuous monitoring of devices and assets connecting to the network is required. This enables implementation of the other tenets, as session-based access is only granted if the Zero Trust engine is aware of the device's security posture.

NIST recommends the implementation of a continuous diagnostics and mitigation (CDM) system to *"monitor the state of devices and applications and should apply patches/fixes as needed. Assets discovered to be subverted, have known vulnerabilities, and are not managed by the enterprise may be treated differently (including denial of all connections to enterprise resources) than devices owned by or associated with the enterprise deemed to be in their most secure state."*

6 - All resource authentication and authorization are dynamic and strictly enforced before access is allowed

NIST loves repeating this, but yes, it re-emphasizes that granting access is dynamic and ongoing. It stresses that *"it is a continuous cycle of scanning devices and assets, using signals for additional insight and evaluating trust decisions before making them. This dynamic process doesn't stop once a user creates an account with *associated resource permissions. It is an iterative process with many factors coming into play with each policy enforcement decision."*

7 - The enterprise collects as much information as possible about the current state of assets, network infrastructure, and communications.

A no-brainer, as it is challenging to secure and make intelligent decisions without having information about what you are trying to secure in the first place!

NIST states, "*An enterprise should collect data about asset security posture, network traffic, and access requests, process that data, and use any insight gained to improve policy creation and enforcement. This data can also provide context for access requests from subjects."*

We will look at this in more detail when we deep dive into the NIST standard, but simply put, the Zero Trust engine needs as much data as possible to improve its decision-making process.

Summing it all up

Zero Trust is understood from the context of its principles only. I hope you better understand these principles and what they require. Remember that they are technology agnostic and can be implemented in various ways in an environment. Now that we have a solid foundation of Zero Trust, its history, and its principles ... let's take a deeper look at the NIST standard and how it approaches Zero Trust.

4 – Understanding the NIST Zero Trust standard

We have already discussed the NIST standard and its tenets-based approach toward Zero Trust. In this chapter, let us dive deeply into how NIST views a Zero Trust architecture and what it considers to be the core components that must be present.

NIST is a great starting point for any company serious about adopting Zero Trust as it is vendor + technology agnostic AND can be adopted by any company. It also focuses on various environments, from on-prem to cloud, and suggests how to implement a ZTA to protect them.

Zero Trust architecture as per NIST

NIST provides a "conceptual architecture" for Zero Trust that can be deployed on-prem or cloud. It consists of several components working together to enforce the Zero Trust tenets/principles we discussed earlier.

The below diagram highlights the same. Let us take at each of these components in detail:

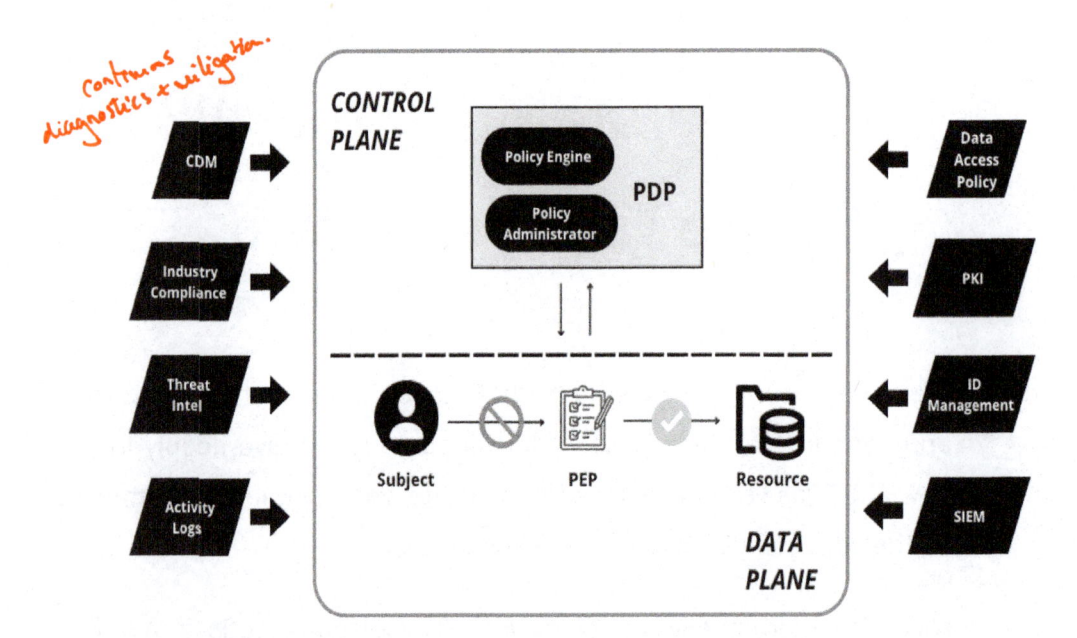

[handwritten annotation: continuous diagnostics + mitigation]

[Diagram showing Control Plane containing Policy Engine and Policy Administrator (PDP), with Data Plane showing Subject → PEP → Resource. Left side inputs: CDM, Industry Compliance, Threat Intel, Activity Logs. Right side inputs: Data Access Policy, PKI, ID Management, SIEM.]

1 - The Control Plane and Data Plane

The concept of a control plane and data plane is familiar in Zero Trust systems. ZTA divides the environment into domains:

39

- **Control Plane:** This is where the Zero Trust engine makes critical decisions. This can be considered the "brains" of the ZTA and thus must be protected from being circumvented or compromised at all costs.
- **Data Plane**: This is where Application Data traffic flows, and the Zero Trust decisions are enforced. This can be considered the "brawn" of the ZTA as it does not make decisions alone but contains the components where the decisions are implemented, such as network firewalls, proxies, and other security solutions.

2 - The Subject and the resource

Every request in a Zero Trust environment revolves around a Subject accessing a Resource over a Data Plane:

- **Subject:** As specified by NIST, this can be a user, an application, or a device that needs access to a resource.
- **Resource**: This is something the Subject needs access to, which can be an application, a workload, or even a document.

The subject requesting access to the resource happens over an untrusted environment and must be granted access through a Policy Enforcement Point (PEP). Let's see how those operate.

3 - The Policy Decision Point (PDP)

The PDP can be referred to as the Zero Trust engine that makes all the decisions. It resides on the Control Plan and consists of two main components:

- **Policy Engine (PE)**: This component makes the final call regarding whether access is granted when a request is made using its Trust algorithm. It makes this decision based on several criteria and data that it collects from supporting systems like the CDM, Threat Intel, etc.
- **Policy Administrator (PA)**: Once the PE makes the decision, the PA is the component that executes the judgment and gives the command to either create or shut down the path between the subject and the resource on the data plane. The PA communicates with the Policy Enforcement Point, which we will read about shortly. If the PE allows it, the PA configures the Policy Enforcement Point to issue a short-lived token or session to enable access. If denied, the PA commands the PEP to shut down the session.

Both these functionalities are combined within the PDP, and they do not have to be separate components in an actual implementation.

4 - The Policy Enforcement Point (PEP)

The PEP is where all the fun happens (not really), but this is the component that acts upon the decisions made by the PDP and either grants or denies access to the resource.

Think of the PEP as a bouncer that allows or disallows people from coming in based on whom the manager trusts at that time.

The PEP gets configured in real-time from the PDP via policy updates. It can be a single component or broken down into multiple, as we will see later when looking at the different variations of ZTA.

5 - Importance of the PDP and PEP

Hearing so many new abbreviations can be a headache, so below is a simplistic representation of how the PDP and the PEP function.

A MORE SIMPLE LOOK

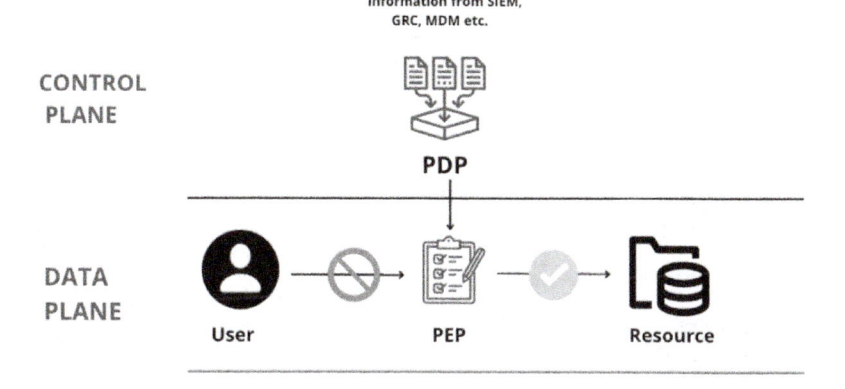

CONTROL PLANE

Information from SIEM, GRC, MDM etc.

PDP

DATA PLANE

User — PEP — Resource

The importance of the PDP and the PEP components must be considered for a genuine Zero Trust Architecture. Placing PDP and PEP in front of every resource makes an environment an actual implementation of a ZTA and differentiates it from traditional networks. These components are how the principles of the ZTA we discussed earlier are enforced, such as authenticating every request and enforcing dynamic policies. They can take different forms and variations, which we will see, but you need to understand the concepts behind them to implement ZTA fully and adequately.

6 - Contextual Data Sources

When deciding whether to allow or disallow access, the PDP refers to several internal and external data sources that feed into its trust engine. Let us look at each of them briefly.

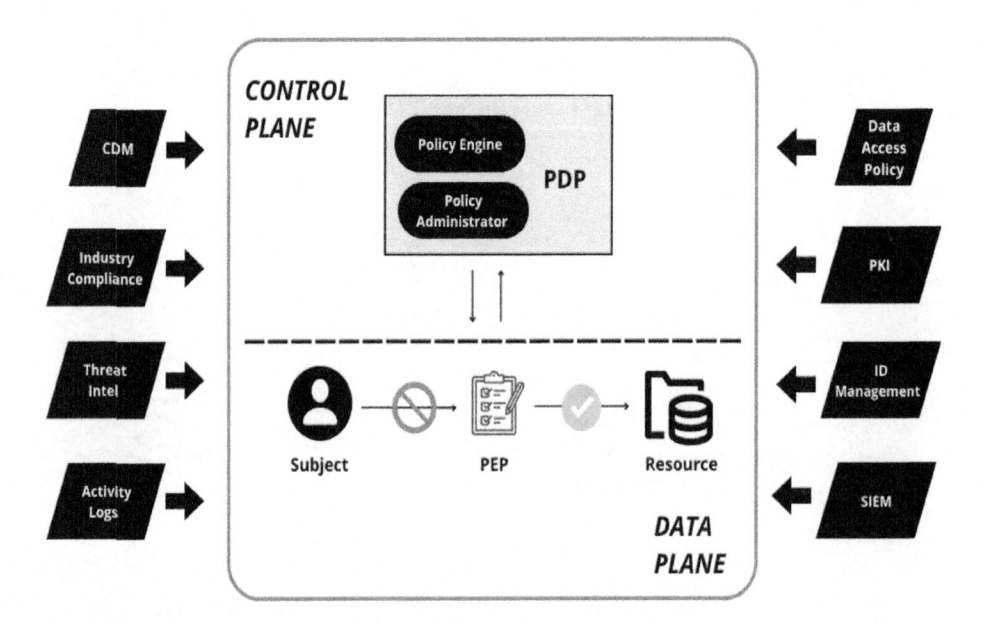

- **Continuous Diagnostics and Mitigation (CDM) system**: The CDM provides input to the Zero Trust engine about device posture, such as patching status, vulnerabilities, unapproved software components, etc. The CDM may also track non-enterprise resources in a BYOD environment.
- **Industry Compliance:** This component contains the

information and rules that the company needs to comply with any regulatory requirements, e.g., PCI DSS, HIPAA, etc.

- **Threat intelligence feed(s)**: As the name applies, this component provides internal and external threat feeds to the Policy Engine about new threats, attacks, and vulnerabilities. This enables the policy engine to remain updated and make intelligent decisions based on the current threat level.
- **Network and system activity logs**: This component gathers records from assets, network traffic, and system activities to provide context to the request being evaluated by the PDP.
- **Data access policies**: Enterprises will have policies defined for their resources per traditional security policies. These rules are provided to the policy engine, forming the starting point for evaluating the request.
- **Enterprise public critical infrastructure (PKI):** As per NIST, *"This system is responsible for generating and logging certificates issued by the enterprise to resources, subjects, services, and applications."*
- **ID management system**: ID management typically stores details about user accounts and identities, such as a Single Sign On (SSO) system. This is where details about the subject (name, email, etc.) will be requested to provide context to the request. Given the nature of modern enterprises, this can be on-prem or on the cloud

and spread across multiple components.
- **Security information and event management (SIEM) system**: A core component of any security architecture, the SIEM contains all security-related logs from the network. This is used to provide the policy engine security-related data about the request.

The last chapter discussed how Zero Trust moves away from binary "allowed / not allowed" access policies to a trust-based algorithm. This trust algorithm is what the PDP uses to decide whether the subject will access the resource or not.

All the data we mentioned earlier is combined with other factors listed below:

- The incoming access request and the subject details are evaluated, such as Operating system, patch level, software, etc. (maybe the requested application is on a blocklist?)
- The subject details, such as what attributes or privileges are present, are also evaluated. For example, does the subject have MFA enabled? Are they coming in from an approved location? Does this fall in line with previously noted behavior? All of these come into play.
- Asset database: The trust algorithm compares what the asset looks like to its historical state before granting or denying access.
- Resource requirements: The access policies defined on the resource being requested. These are the minimum baseline requirements that must be satisfied and are usually

determined by the data custodian.

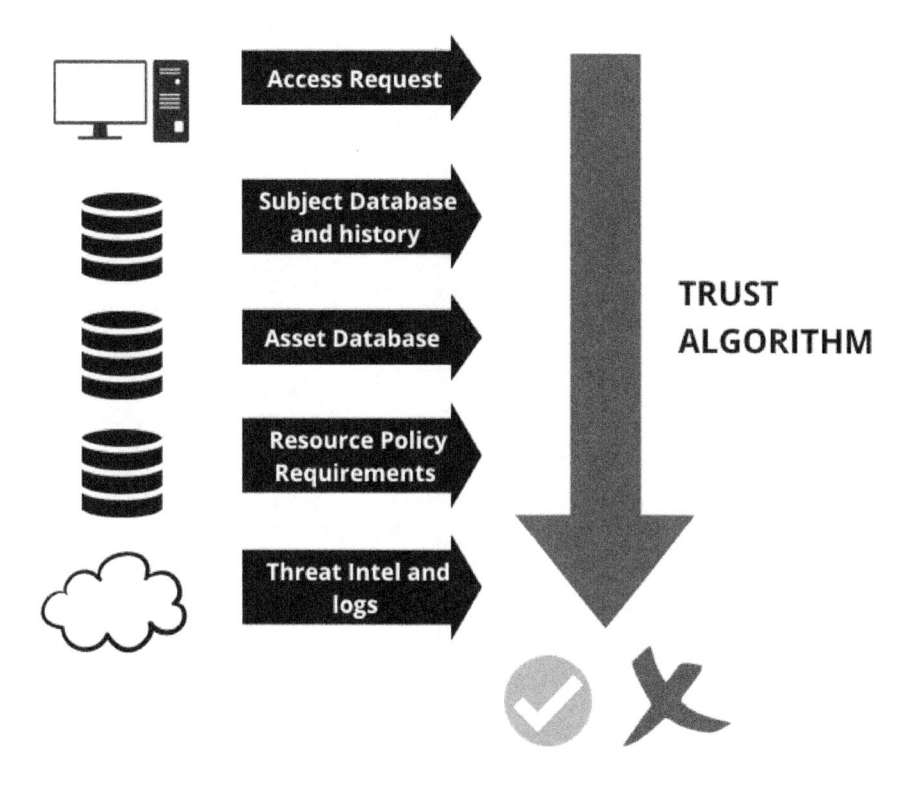

[Diagram: Access Request, Subject Database and history, Asset Database, Resource Policy Requirements, Threat Intel and logs → TRUST ALGORITHM → ✓ / ✗]

How important each of these factors is given can be defined by the algorithm or configurable by the enterprise. Once the trust algorithm has made the decision, it passes it onto the PEP for execution and implementation.

Summing it all up

In this chapter, we moved away from abstract high principles to a more detailed look at how Zero Trust Architecture would get implemented. In the next chapter, we will look at a few variations of this architecture that accommodates different real-world scenarios you might encounter.

5 – Zero Trust variations and models

In the previous chapter, we discussed the roles of the PDP, PEP, and control/data plane in setting up an actual Zero Trust environment. Let us now look at a few of the variations that are present.

Companies and networks are unique, so it stands to reason that no two Zero Trust architectures will be the same. NIST and other documents referencing ZTA deliberately keep it high level to accommodate any environment, as every company will implement the concept of the PDP and PEP differently.

NIST takes this into account and provides the following guidance in its document:

- High-level architectural approaches for Zero Trust strategies

- Deployment variations about how the PDP and the PEP should be implemented.
- Business-level scenarios that consider how companies are structured.

Let us look at each of them briefly.

A - NIST architecture approaches

These are high-level strategies for how Zero Trust should be implemented.

1 - Enhanced Identity Governance

In this strategic approach, the company focuses the Zero Trust strategy on Identities and how they are governed. Factors like users' privilege and their current risk score are the core focus of policy decisions to grant or disallow access. While other factors like device security can be considered, they are not the core factor. This form of zero trust strategy is centralized within a single or a combination of identity stores.

2 - Micro-Segmentation

We discussed microsegmentation earlier and how it builds upon the concept of network segmentation. In a microsegmentation zero trust approach, software-defined parameters control access to critical resources, configured dynamically by the zero trust engine. So, the firewalls and gateway components play the part of the PEP in this decentralized model compared to the previous approach.

NEED FOR MICROSEGMENTATION

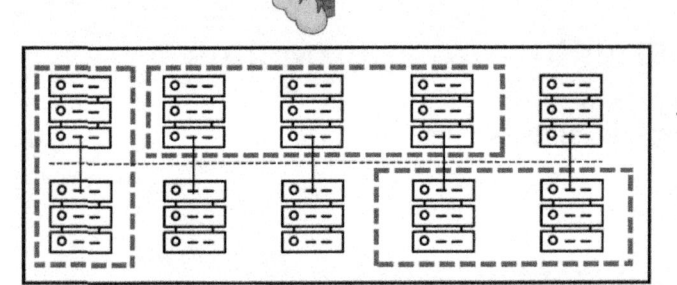

Sensitive subnet WITH microsegmentation

3 - Network Infrastructure & Software-Defined Perimeters

This is like the microsegmentation approach, but at a higher level, as in this scenario, the network is dynamically configured to allow or disallow connections. The software-defined perimeter can be configured like an overlay network the PDP configures.

Which is the best approach?

There is no right or wrong approach, as it depends on each company's overall strategy and technology stack. Plan your strategy and what plays to your company's strengths and technical solutions.

B - NIST deployed variations

Deployed variations are NIST guidance on how to set up the PDP and PEP in different scenarios. These are low-level and provide tactical advice on where to place the components.

1 - Device Agent/Gateway-Based

In this deployment, the PEP is composed of two agents, one that sits on the subject side and one that sits with the resource. These communicate with each other at request time, and PEP on the resource end is responsible for communicating with the PEP on the subject end as per the following diagram. Given the dynamic configurations possible in this approach, this approach works with the microsegmentation and software perimeter approach.

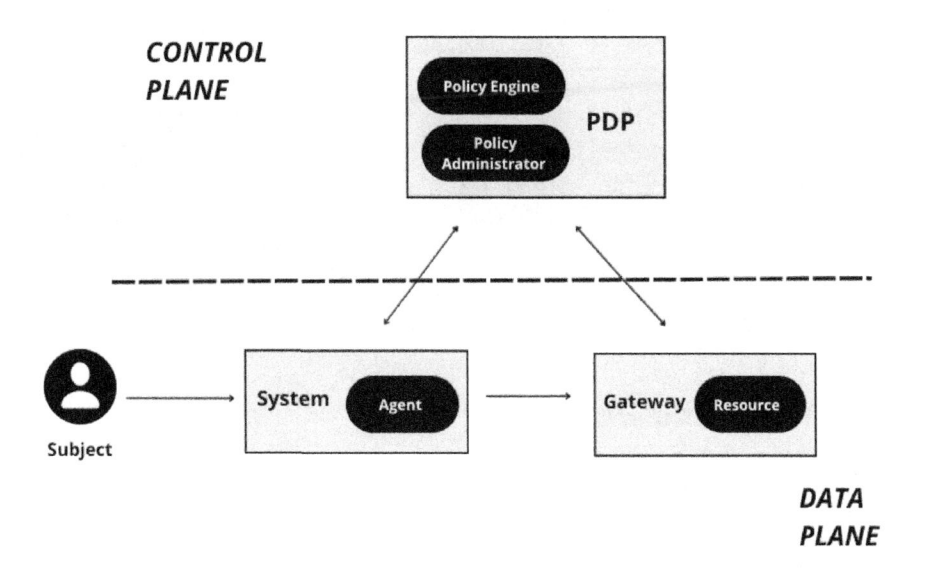

2 - Enclave-Based

In the enclave model, the deployment is like the previous one, except a gateway on the resource side protects many resources instead of the 1-1 mapping we saw in the last model. Once the user has been authenticated, they can access the resources within the enclave. This is good for environments that might not support all the Zero Trust principles and allows us to implement a bit of a hybrid approach as potentially there is implied trust here.

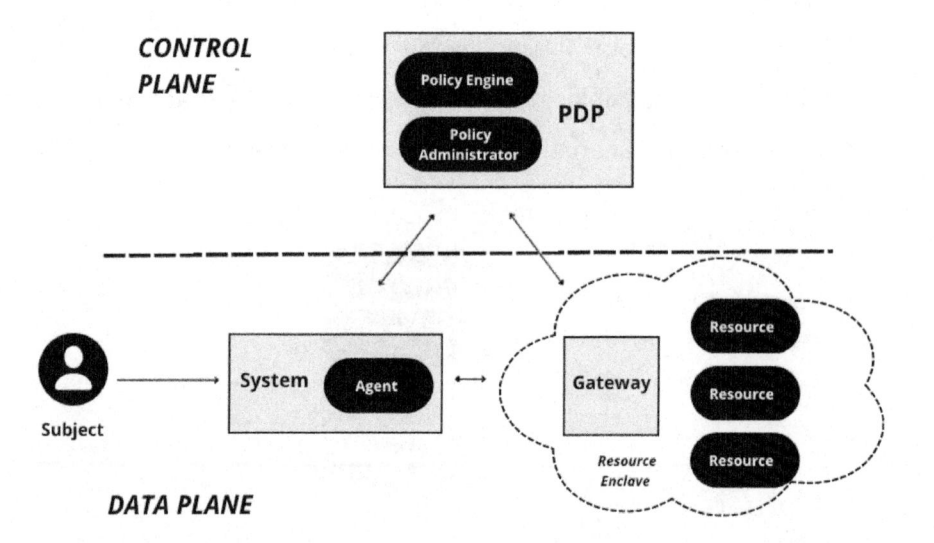

3 - Resource Portal

This deployment is comparatively centralized, with one system representing the PEP for all assets (or a large group). This approach has the advantage of flexibility since it does not require agents on all client assets, which is excellent for a BYOD environment. Still, compared with other approaches, it limits visibility and control over user postures and actions. The PEP can only know how secure a device is once it has connected to it and will not be able to continuously monitor their compliance due to a lack of agents.

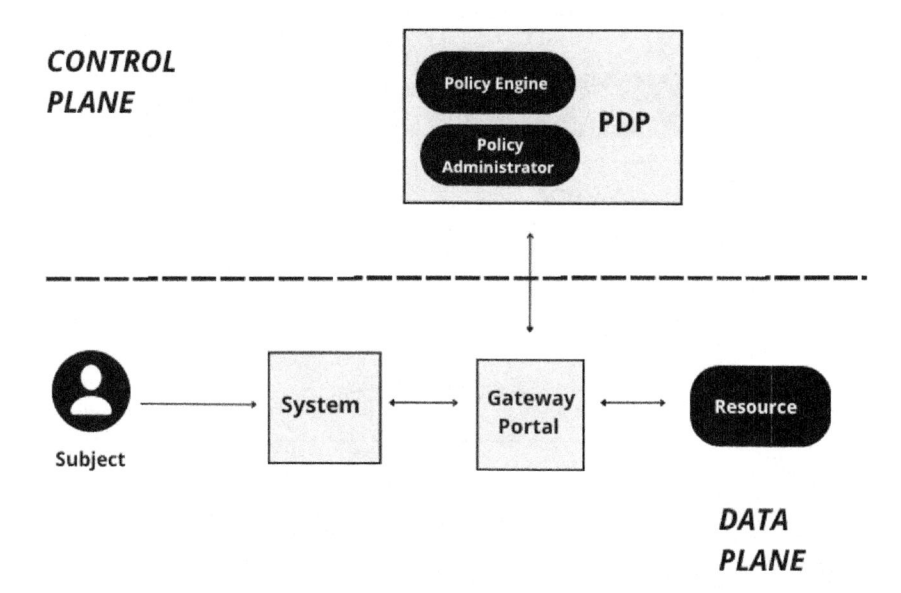

CONTROL PLANE

Policy Engine
Policy Administrator
PDP

Subject → System ↔ Gateway Portal ↔ Resource

DATA PLANE

The Gateway portal itself can become a point of attack and hence must be highly secured and hardened against potential security risks.

4 - Device Application Sandboxing

This approach uses sandboxing technology, such as virtualization or containers, to run authorized applications only. The PEP will allow requests from specific applications on a device or asset and disapprove others.

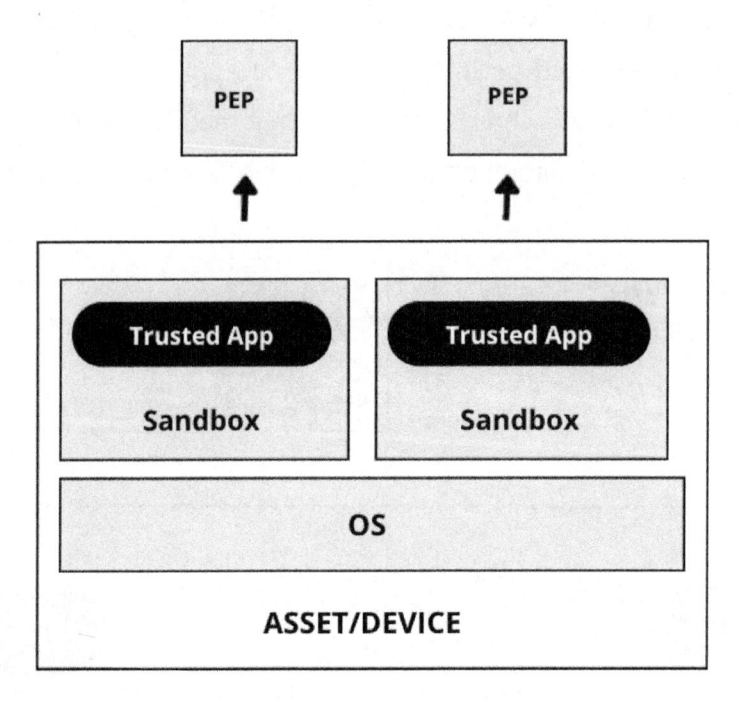

```
           [PEP]           [PEP]
             ↑               ↑
  ┌──────────────────────────────────────┐
  │  ┌──────────────┐   ┌──────────────┐ │
  │  │ Trusted App  │   │ Trusted App  │ │
  │  │   Sandbox    │   │   Sandbox    │ │
  │  └──────────────┘   └──────────────┘ │
  │  ┌──────────────────────────────────┐│
  │  │               OS                 ││
  │  └──────────────────────────────────┘│
  │             ASSET/DEVICE             │
  └──────────────────────────────────────┘
```

Sandboxing prevents the applications on the device from being compromised if the host device or surrounding application gets compromised. This is useful for scenarios where the company does not have control over device posture and cannot continuously monitor them but still needs to ensure its applications are secure.

C - Zero Trust scenarios

Zero Trust scenarios from NIST are very high-level examples of how Zero Trust would be implemented in different environments. They help visualize practical implementations of ZTA for stakeholders.

1 - Enterprise with Satellite Facilities

In this scenario, you would have an enterprise headquarters with several branch offices or remote workers. Remote users can easily be granted access, but more critical assets are restricted to on-premises access only.

The PDP in this scenario would be in the cloud, while the PEP will either follow the agent-based or a portal approach.

Architecting the ZTA in this way would mean the remote workers do not need to access the on-prem network every time they need to authenticate and can access the Cloud Service for assessment.

2 - Multi-Cloud/Cloud-to-Cloud Enterprise

Multi-cloud is becoming increasingly popular amongst enterprises that segregate critical workloads amongst two or more cloud providers.

If an application in Cloud A wants to access a resource in Cloud B, making a round trip back to an on-prem infrastructure for security verification and wasting bandwidth will not make sense. Thus, in this scenario, it would not make sense to place the PDP on-prem; instead, a cloud-based PDP would be used.

Like the previous model, every device can have a PEP agent or connect to a PEP portal to get access. This would let the enterprise control access even to outside resources.

3 - Contracted Services/Nonemployee Access

Most organizations commonly have contractor and partner access, and NIST caters to this scenario. Partners might need limited internet access or network connectivity to do their job but do not need access to corporate resources like applications or databases.

Zero Trust could be architected so that company employees can access resources as needed through a PEP (agent or resource-based). Contractors would only get limited access and be denied corporate resources due to insufficient credentials or an agent installed.

A cloud-based PDP is unnecessary in this scenario and can also be located on-prem.

4 - Collaboration across Enterprise Boundaries

Companies often need to collaborate with other parties and provide access to their employees. In this scenario, company A providing access would require employees from company B to validate with either an agent-based PEP or a resource-based one. The PDP should be in the cloud, allowing company A to mitigate risks without drastically changing its architecture.

5 - Enterprise with Public/Customer-Facing Services

This is a unique situation in which the company has no control over the security posture of the asset. In this scenario, the company has resources accessed by investments that are entirely beyond its control. NIST recommends heavily relying on behavior metrics to determine the security posture of incoming requests and using a resource-based PEP.

D - Zero Trust Threats

Cybersecurity risks can exist in any scenario, and Zero Trust is no exception. While an adequately implemented ZTA can significantly reduce your risk profile, it introduces new risks you must know about. NIST highlights the following.

1 - Bypass the decision process

A fundamental principle in the ZTA decision process is that access should only happen via PEP, which checks with the PDP about whether to allow or disallow access. However, what if there were connections or ways to access the resource without going through the PEP? Or what if the administrators who handle the policy decision-making process added exceptions without an authorization? It is also possible for the PDP to get compromised and malicious changes made, allowing attackers to introduce their exceptions to the decision-making process.

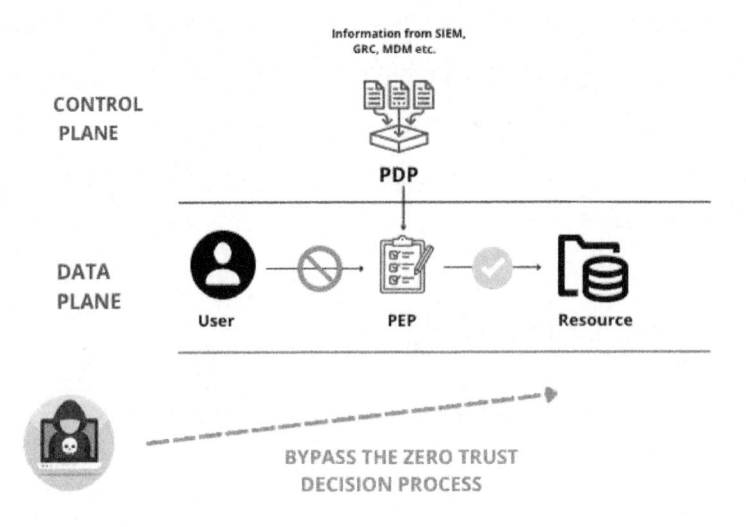

Such risks can be mitigated by hardening the Zero Trust engine, ensuring the Control Plane is not accessible except via authorized means, and monitoring policy changes.

2 - Make the PDP or PEP unavailable

In this scenario, an attacker might no longer be interested in compromising the PDP or the PEP and might focus on making it unavailable. Given that these components mediate access, an attack on them might lead to a service outage or a denial-of-service attack. Architecting the PDP to be resilient to such attacks (multiple cloud regions) and following best practices for cyber resilience can help mitigate such attacks. This type of risk has existed for critical systems since the dawn of the Internet, and Zero Trust is no exception. But it should be ensured that the PDP and PEP can handle the network load, as you want to avoid this disruption happening just from regular traffic!

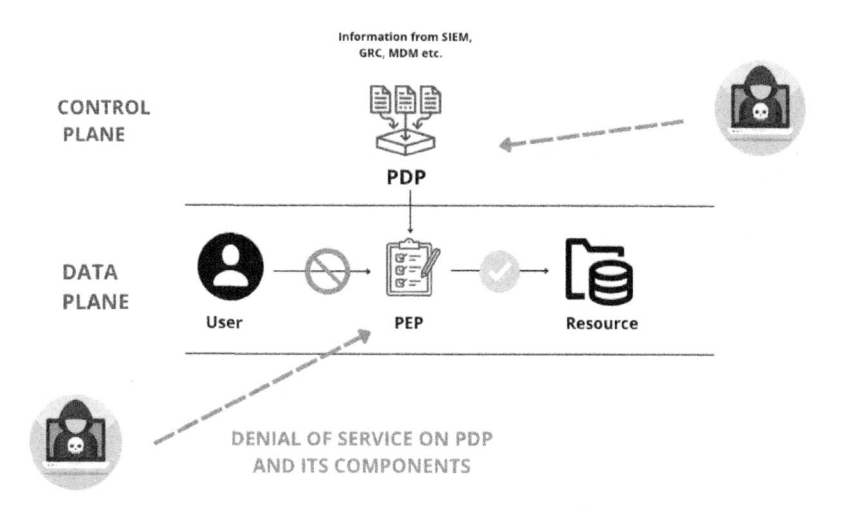

3 - Stolen credentials

Cybercriminals are not a stupid bunch, and they will adapt to Zero Trust Architectures just like they have adapted to every cybersecurity control introduced. As they realize how ZTA counters the risk of implicit trust, they will focus on compromising legitimate devices/credentials and their MFA tokens. Again, while ZTA will significantly reduce the blast radius of such attacks and limit lateral movement, this attack is still possible. As ZTA integrates more and more with AI-driven controls that can baseline user behavior, we should be able to reduce the risk of such attacks.

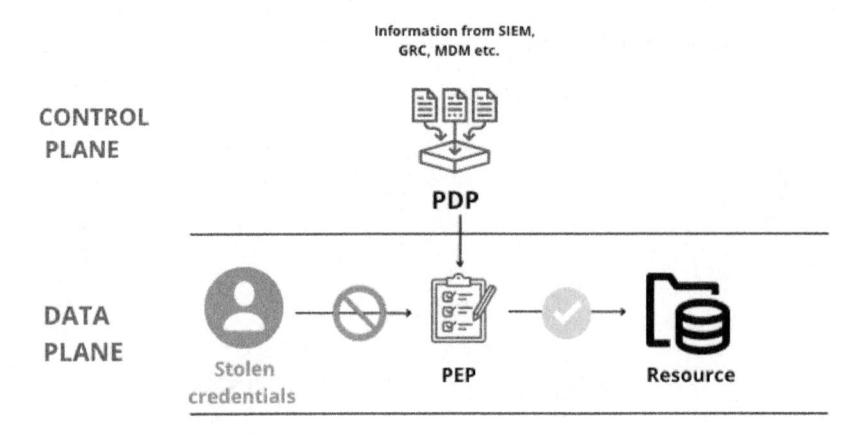

4 - Lack of visibility

The ability to log and inspect traffic is critical for the PDP to decide to allow or disallow access. Zero Trust components might not have the required visibility on the network due to unsupported traffic or personal devices not supporting a particular solution. However, it might be possible to use Metadata about such requests and rely on Machine Learning powered security solutions that baseline behavior to compensate.

5 - Storage of sensitive information

We discussed the trust algorithm in the Zero Trust Engine and how it uses data from multiple sources to form a decision. This data can be a goldmine for attackers wishing to gain information about decisions and how to subvert them.

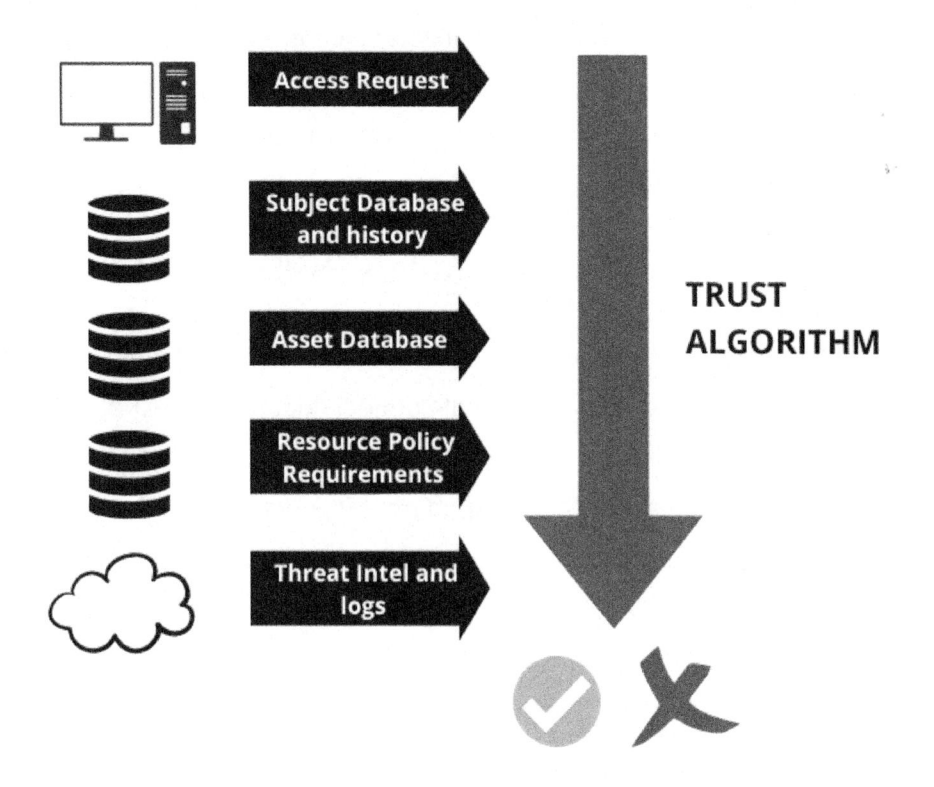

```
                    Access Request →
 [PC]
                    Subject Database
                    and history →
 [DB]                                    TRUST
                    Asset Database →    ALGORITHM
 [DB]
                    Resource Policy
                    Requirements →
 [DB]
                                         ↓
                    Threat Intel and
 [cloud]            logs →

                                        ✓  ✗
```

The same applies to the access policies which the PDP uses to make decisions. If an attacker can view these policies, they can gain information about bypassing them or which accounts are the most valuable targets to compromise. These Zero Trust components must be hardened per security best practices and protected from attack.

6 - Vendor lock-in

Although not a risk that is unique to Zero Trust, it is possible that in their eagerness, companies might implement black box ZTA solutions and get locked into specific vendors for the long term. In such a scenario, a key or architecture change can be costly and effort intensive once a ZTA has been implemented. It is essential for companies adopting Zero Trust to consider these factors beforehand and consider the cost and effort required for future changes.

8 - Use of non-person entities (NPE) in ZTA

A ZTA comprises multiple components that work together without human input to form a full-fledged ecosystem. For these components to interact and query with each other, authentication mechanisms must be set up, such as API keys, certificates, service accounts, etc., the security of which is critical. An attacker could try to piggyback on such authentication, compromise them, or trick them into performing a task on their behalf.

Chapter Summary

In this chapter, we saw the flexibility and variations of Zero Trust Architecture and how it can accommodate different scenarios and requirements. Due to pre-existing security best practices, most companies have some form of Zero Trust capabilities within their environments. It is just a matter of aligning them to the model. The approaches, variations, and scenarios that NIST provides are a great source of guidance for companies new to their Zero Trust journey but remember that there is no "one size fits all" for implementing a true ZTA.

We also saw some of the threats and risks in a ZTA and why this should be considered when designing an architecture or choosing a solution.

6 – A Zero Trust case study

We can talk about Zero Trust concepts and principles all day, but we will only learn if we implement those principles in an actual scenario. In this chapter, we will look at a company that wants to implement Zero Trust and see how we would implement some of the architecture and concepts we discussed earlier.

Company ABC

Tom is a CISO at Company ABC. He has matured and implemented the cybersecurity framework at ABC over several years and is quite proud of it.

ABC has many remote workers that connect over a VPN, and it is slowly moving towards a hybrid cloud environment as the CIO is quite fond of infrastructure as code. They have started putting non-critical workloads on the cloud connected to the on-prem environment via a dedicated VPN. Multiple firewalls are present at the DMZ and Internal network layers.

A few of Tom's key security achievements during his time as the CISO are:

- Segmenting off mission-critical applications in their network segment
- Implementing a Security Information and Event Management (SIEM) tool for security events and alerts the security team monitors.
- Enforcing Single Sign On so all users authenticate towards a single source.
- Implementing a Privileged Identity Management (PIM) solution that controls admin sessions and enforces multi-factor authentication.

In a nutshell, a high-level overview of Company ABC would look like the following:

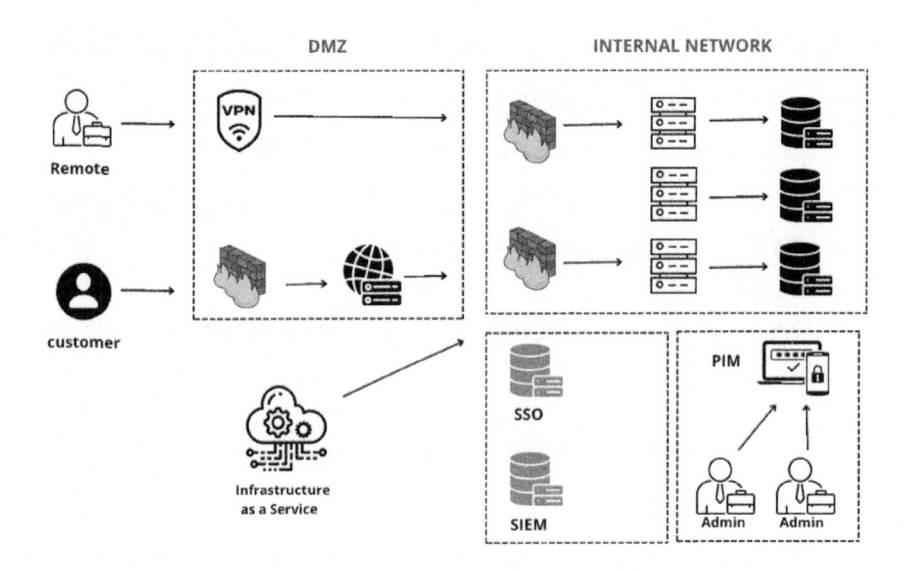

The CIO is keen on moving everyone towards remote work and wants to stop worrying about who is accessing what from where and from which device. He wants to go all-in into the cloud and wants Tom to find a way to secure all of this while giving him the flexibility he needs.

Tom thinks the CIO is moving WAY too fast but wants to be someone other than the guy that says NO to everything. He also knows remote work and cloud-first is the future of Company ABC. Tom has read up on Zero Trust and thinks this is the way to go to future-proof the cybersecurity framework of his company.

Tom has interviewed and hired YOU as the information security manager. Your mandate is quite simple. Start Company ABC on the journey towards Zero Trust using the NIST standard as a guideline. Tom knows it is a long-term journey, but he needs a high-level architecture and roadmap, so the ball starts moving toward Zero

Trust.

Oh, and by the way, there is zero budget for this as no one had any idea what to put in for a Zero Trust implementation.

Good luck!

Step 1 - Assessing the architecture.

We talked before about how Zero Trust is not a product and how most companies are not starting from scratch when it comes to Zero Trust. Some of those principles exist in all environments, and Company ABC is no exception. Tom, as the CISO has built a strong cybersecurity baseline, it is up to you to refine it further and successfully deploy a Zero Trust architecture.

When it comes to implementing Zero Trust, you can already see some questions that need answering:

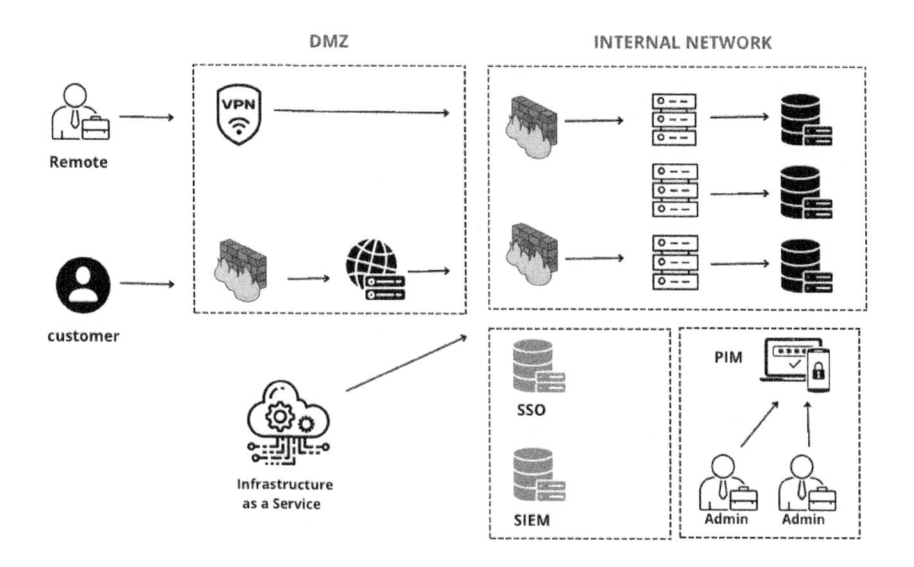

- *How do you structure it so that remote workers are authenticated regardless of which device they are using?*
- *Mission-critical applications are segmented, but what about once access is granted to an admin via the PIM? There is some implicit trust going on in the internal network.*
- *Where to put the Zero Trust engine? i.e., which component would be acting as the control plan here that houses the PDP?*
- *How and where to put the Policy Enforcement Points (PEP) and what devices would use.*
- *Is the Cloud missing a firewall component to protect traffic from the internal network? How to enforce Zero Trust in the cloud?*

If we remember Zero Trust architecture at a high level, then remember this is how it looks like:

ZERO TRUST DEPLOYMENT

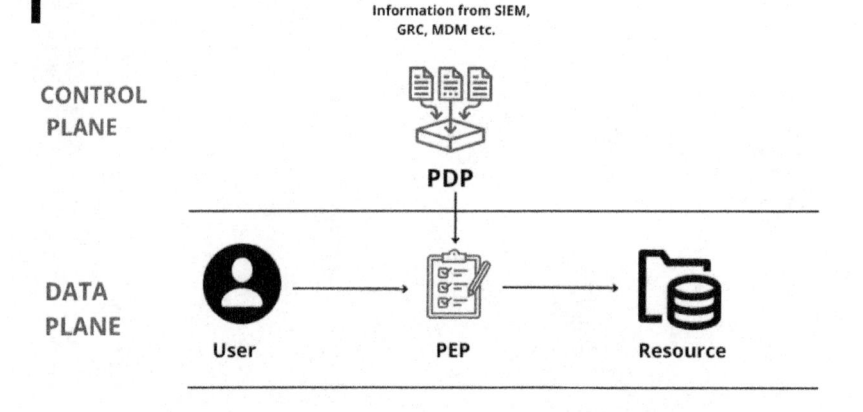

Information from SIEM, GRC, MDM etc.

CONTROL PLANE

PDP

DATA PLANE

User → PEP → Resource

The first decision would be where to place the PDP and PEP in this architecture.

Step 2 - Deciding upon the PDP

The PDP is the brains behind Zero Trust decisions and can be a product that you implement or an in-house developed system. As we saw earlier, the key is that it must make intelligent decisions from different data sources. You can either use existing security products that you have or build a custom solution from scratch, but it should have the following:

- Ability to define fine-tuned and granular policies that cover the conditions under which users, applications, and devices can access resources.
- Ability to gather contextual information about users, devices, network, time of access, etc., and utilize it in decision-making.
- Have a policy engine in place that allows it to execute these policies against contextual information.
- The mechanism must be highly secured and resilient to attacks and threats.

In your opinion, the best solution for the PDP would be the organization's SSO solution. It already contains a custom policy engine that meets the requirements highlighted above and resides in a particular segment that meets the need of the control plane.

The PDP must decide about users and devices before

allowing/disallowing them. It can make such decisions by the data it gathers when users/devices authenticate and via a custom integration with the SIEM solution that the vendor should be able to provide. The SIEM vendor will happily offer this integration which is great news. Querying the SIEM about the status of security posture through API integration and then making intelligent policy decisions about the same should meet the initial requirements of Zero Trust. For the PIM, the vendor is willing to integrate, but there is a high cost involved for any changes, so you note this down for further discussion.

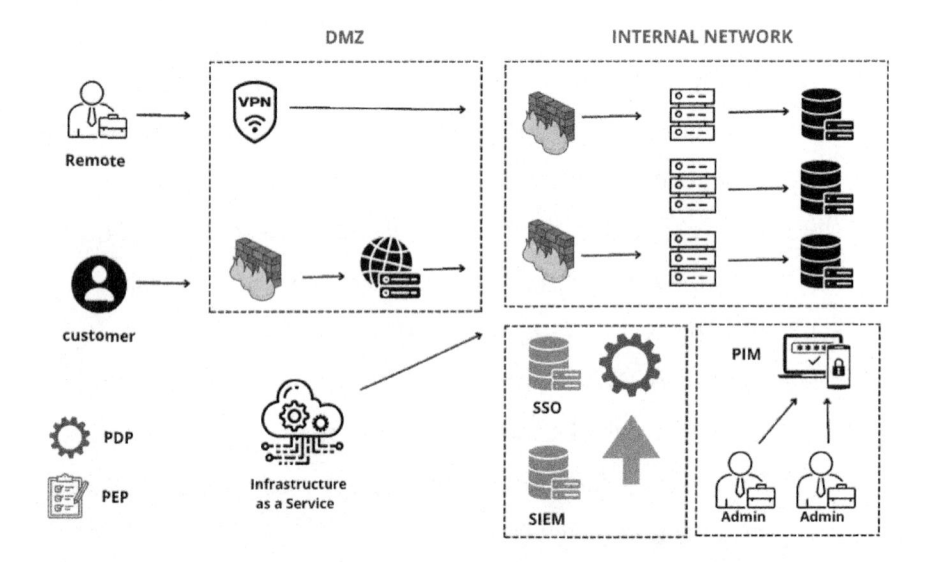

Step 3 - Deciding upon the PEP

The PDP will not be able to do if it does not have PEP components to enforce its policy decisions. You decide that multiple PEPs must be present throughout this architecture so that the Zero Trust Engine governs access. The network devices already current in the infrastructure, such as the Firewalls, seem like a perfect choice to carry out the function of the PEPs in each segment and enforce the policy decisions. The same goes for the VPN solution through which remote workers connect.

You provided an updated diagram to the CISO showing where the PDP and the PEP should be placed in the new architecture.

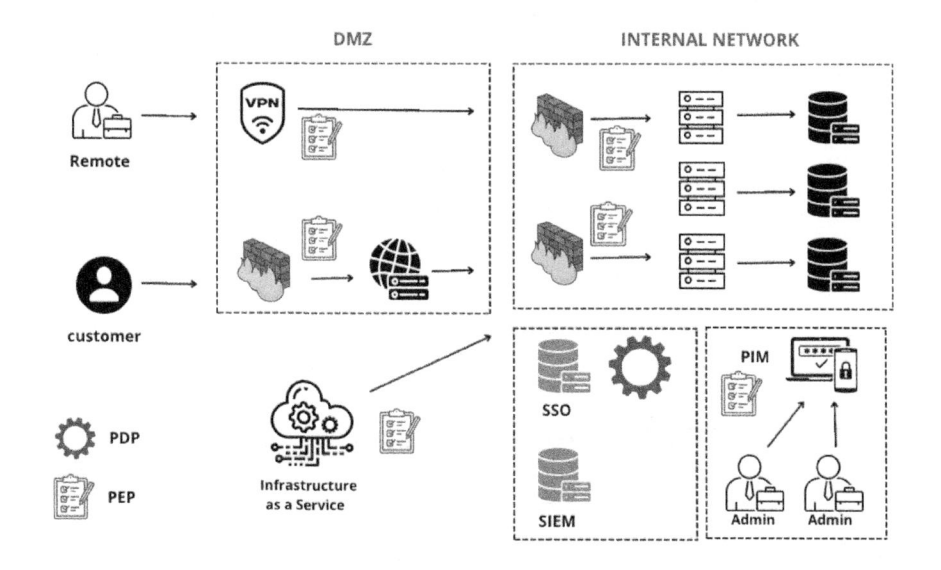

This architecture will present the PDP in the same secure segment as the SIEM and SSO solutions. The feature will function as the Control Plane and the PDP will make policy decisions based on the data gathered from these two security components.

The PEPs will be present at network entry points such as the VPN, Cloud infrastructure, Internal Firewalls, PIM, etc., and enforce its context-based decisions. The PDP will configure the firewall policies dynamically to implement its findings and make it perform the function of the PEP.

In theory, it would function like the below diagram.

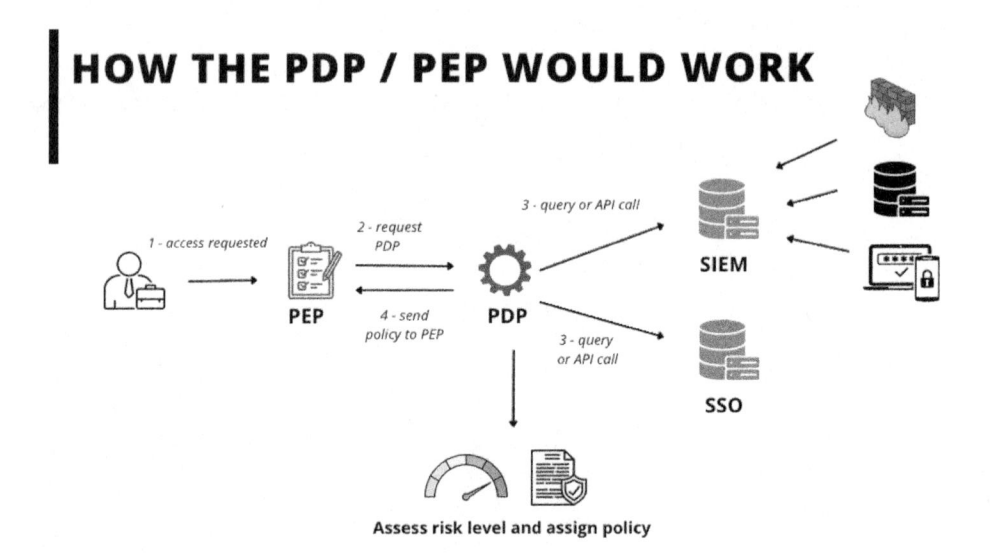

HOW THE PDP / PEP WOULD WORK

1 - access requested
2 - request PDP
3 - query or API call
4 - send policy to PEP
PEP
PDP
SIEM
3 - query or API call
SSO
Assess risk level and assign policy

Step 4 - What about microsegmentation

One problem you can see is that there is a lot of implicit once the admins authenticate via the PIM. As per Zero Trust principles, there should be more boundaries between workloads in the internal segment to stop lateral movement in case of a breach, and microsegmentation is the answer.

You sit down with the application team to understand which admin needs access to which workload to create logical boundaries for who needs access to what server. Certain admins do not need to access specific workloads like servers and databases, and further segmentation can be implemented, which will look like the following diagram.

INTERNAL NETWORK

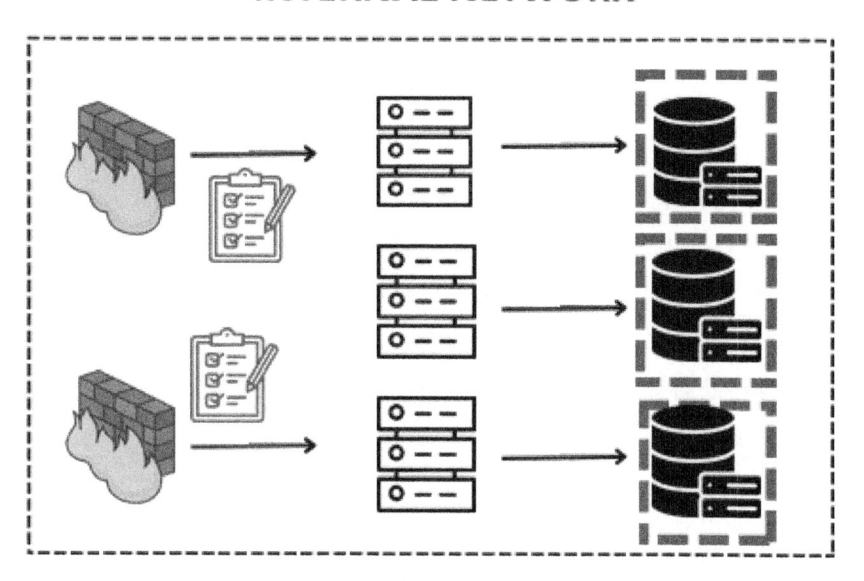

The challenge, unfortunately, is that currently, there is no solution to implement microsegmentation in the environment and re-architecting the internal network by creating / reconfiguring VLANs will take a massive amount of effort. Another problem is that most rules are expressed in terms of network details, i.e., allow access from this IP address/ disallow access from this IP, etc., and do not look into tags or attributes of the workloads which will enable intelligent microsegmentation to happen.

For properly implementing microsegmentation, you need a solution that will have visibility into traffic and impose rules based on context. Changes to workload attributes should trigger changes at runtime without any admin input.

You know agent-based and agentless solutions for microsegmentation are available, but a cost investment will be required for licensing, etc. You make a mental note to discuss this with the CISO later.

Step 5 - The Cloud environment

The Cloud environment is being used for non-critical workloads for the time being, but this is only temporary. You know that the CIO is a cloud-first person who wants to move critical workloads to the cloud as soon as possible.

The good news is that cloud workloads are authenticating to the SSO, so the PDP will have access and be able to make decisions on incoming requests.

The bad news is that due to the workloads being non-critical, no firewall was implemented between the internal and cloud environments.

What to do about the PEP in this case?

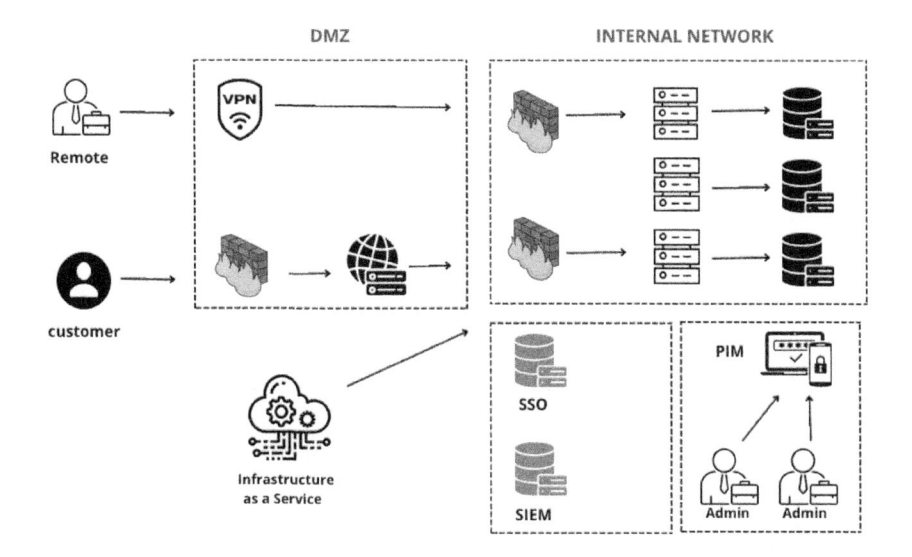

After some digging, you learn about native cloud capabilities, such as **network security groups** that are dynamically configurable at runtime.

Workloads in the cloud can easily be tagged with attributes like "production" and "non-production," These tags can be used to change network security in real-time.

This is excellent news and means that PEP capabilities can be implemented in the cloud along with a basic form of microsegmentation!

Step 6 - Presenting to the CISO for feedback.

You create a high-level presentation of the Zero Trust architecture and where the components would fit and present the same to Tom. You highlight the PDP and PEP placements and how microsegmentation could be implemented in future stages.

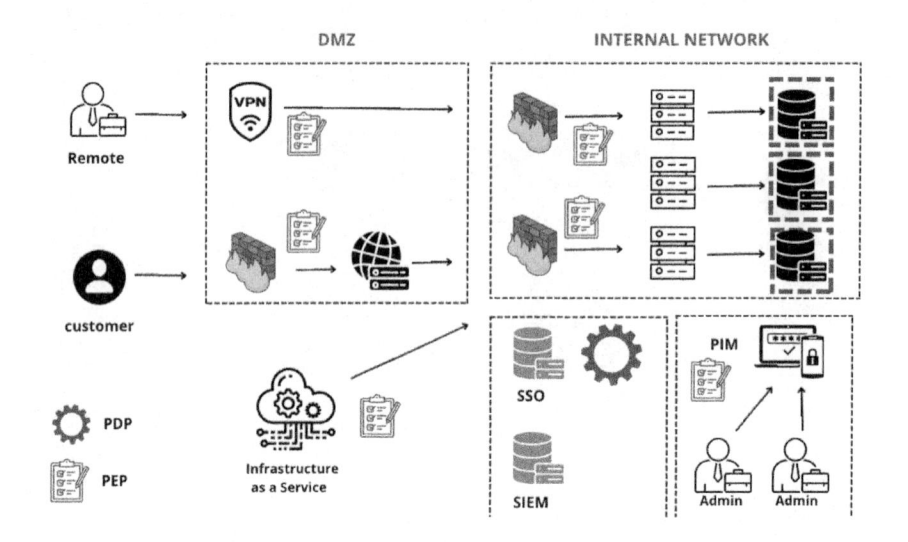

You also highlight how the PDP would work and get details from the SIEM and maybe the PIM in the future before authorizing any requests.

The firewalls in the on-prem network would act as the PEPs, and the cloud's network security groups will be used both as a PEP and for implementing a basic form of microsegmentation.

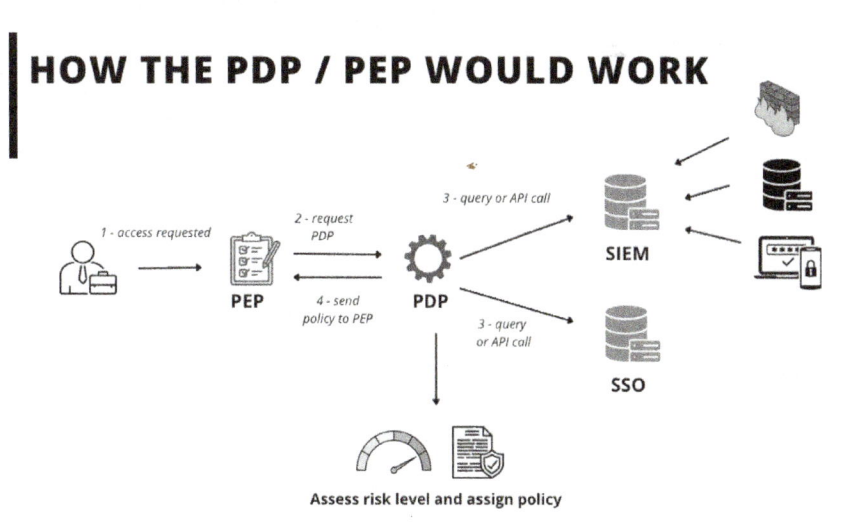

HOW THE PDP / PEP WOULD WORK

Tom has a few concerns about using the firewall components as the PEP and has the following questions:

- Can our firewalls dynamically enforce the PDP instructions?
- Do they even have support for active policies and configurations?
- How much network change will the PDP component need to communicate securely with the PEP devices?

He informs you that some of the network components are old, and there will be a performance impact if the policies are routinely changed, and it must enforce context-driven policies.

This is a challenge you did not expect, as a device can only be considered a PEP if it can dynamically respond to policy decisions from the PDP and update itself automatically.

You analyze the network firewall devices, specifically checking if they support dynamic policy configuration and can handle the extra load from the PDP.

The good news is that many firewalls are newly implemented and can support these functions. However, some devices have not been replaced for some time and do not meet the requirements. Dynamic policy configuration cannot be implemented on them and needs manual input, which defeats the purpose of implementing a Zero Trust model in the first place.

You return to the CISO with a list of network devices needing replacement and a roadmap for transitioning these devices.

The CISO knows that Zero Trust is not a big-bang approach, will need to mature over time, and agrees with you. He is happy with implementing initial microsegmentation on the cloud and using it as a testing place for more dynamic policies. He will need to budget for replacing the older network devices and the microsegmentation solution for internal workloads. However, given its benefits, he is confident the CIO will be more than happy to provide.

Your Zero Trust roadmap

After various discussions, you and Tom have decided upon the below phase-wise approach for Zero Trust implementation.

Phase 1 - Putting a foundation.

- Decide on the Zero Trust rules the PDP will enforce for remote users, admins, and cloud applications.

- Enforce changes in the SSO to make it function as the PDP and integrate with the SIEM solution for further intelligence.
- Start testing network firewalls in the on-prem network for dynamic firewall policy configuration and set up a secure path for communication with the PDP.
- Implement tagging for cloud resources and create functions in the cloud that will get triggered based on any attribute changes. These functions will dynamically change the network security groups on these workloads.
- Assess the cost of replacing network devices, PIM integration with PDP, and a microsegmentation solution!

Phase 2 - Filling in the gaps

- Replace the older network devices to implement the PEP component fully.
- Implement microsegmentation solutions for internal network workloads. Tom wants a solution that can work on-prem and on the cloud so that minimum changes will be required. He prefers an agent-based solution that can extract attributes from the workloads at runtime and dynamically change network rules in response.
- Initiate testing of BYOD Policies against the PDP and see how non-corporate devices can be controlled.
- Integrate the PIM with the SSO solution so the PDP can make more intelligent decisions by analyzing admin-based logs.

Not a perfect plan by any means but you and Tom are happy and excited to be starting on this journey!

Summing it all up

In this chapter, we saw a high-level overview of a potential Zero Trust implementation and the challenges that come with it. As I have repeatedly stated, given how many different variations are present. There is no magical "one size fits all" solution to Zero Trust.

Yet still, we saw a high-level representation and an essential roadmap. In the coming chapters, we will cover the threats to Zero Trust and how to create and mature a Zero Trust implementation in a company.

7 – How to start a Zero Trust Project

In the previous chapter, we got a rough idea of how Zero Trust architecture would get implemented in a company. The entire scenario, however, assumed that Zero Trust is something the company wants and that the CISO has full support for. This is usually not the case, however, and Zero Trust is something that management must be convinced of before you get the green light to start implementing.

Always remember the below:

- Zero Trust is a significant investment of time and money, so focus on small wins to show management the return they are getting.
- It is a journey on which you will mature over time. We will see a few sample maturity levels in this chapter.

ZERO TRUST JOURNEY

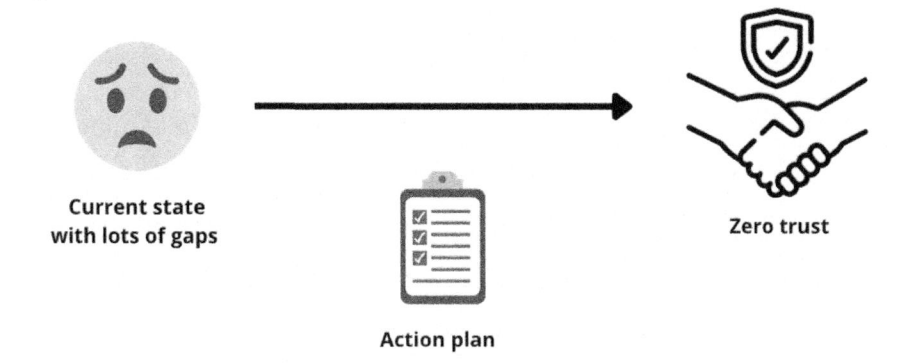

Current state with lots of gaps → Action plan → Zero trust

At a high level, implementing Zero Trust in any company from scratch involves the following steps:

1. Get management buy-in
2. Understand and map the environment.
3. Introduce control mechanisms.
4. Implement the zero trust model.
5. Maintain, monitor, and improve the model.

1 - Get management buy in

Unfortunately, this old cliche is true for nearly every project, and Zero Trust is no exception. You need management support if you want your Zero Trust project to get off the ground. Get an executive sponsor, be it the CIO, CEO, or COO, and get their buy-in by showing them the benefits of a proper Zero Trust implementation.

Zero Trust is a journey that needs a lot of effort and cost (both financial and non-financial), so this will be invaluable in the long run.

Identify your executive sponsor and pitch the Zero Trust implementation to them with the following features:

- What security measures do you already have in place, and how will Zero Trust benefit?
- The Zero Trust roadmap and the incremental improvements it will bring. Refrain from focusing too much on the technical aspects but show why Zero Trust is needed.
- Be upfront about the changes needed to the current way of doing things and the potential issues and challenges.
- Include a ballpark figure of the cost that is involved.

If you have a project management office, set it up as a proper project that is monitored and reported on such accountability is also there. It is also essential to set up an appropriate committee of stakeholders from IT, Security, Risk, Audit, and other governance areas overseeing this project.

By the end of this phase, you should have:

- Management buy-in
- A governance committee setup for your Zero Trust project with defined ownership
- A clear roadmap and vision for how Zero Trust will look like

2 - Understand and map the environment

At this stage, you have gotten the green light from management and are starting your Zero Trust journey.

The first step would be to map your environment and discover the critical assets, devices, capabilities, etc. A foundational ability of Zero Trust is to be able to identify devices and users and whether they are corporate or non-corporate.

Make sure you cover the following:

- User and Service accounts and their level of privilege
- Applications
- Mobile Devices (personal and corporate)
- Laptops and workstations
- Digital certificates
- Servers
- Cloud platforms and services

Ideally, this information should be available with IT, but in more cases than not, only a partial inventory is available. You might have to query and collate this information from multiple sources, such as:

- A configuration management database (CMDB)
- Active directory or similar authentication store
- Mobile Device Management Solution (MDM)

Zero Trust must quickly identify and assess new assets and resources as they become available and implement controls.

Suppose there is no way to get all this information. In that case, I recommend investing or building the capability to get an inventory of all users and assets, which will be critical later.

This could be a single sign-on (SSO), a Mobile Device Management Solution (MDM), or a combination of those and a third-party solution. But remember, we need these capabilities when applying security decisions, so the result of this phase should be the ability to carry out the following:

- Discover a new asset, whether a user, application, or resource, when it connects. It does not matter whether it is corporate or non-corporate.
- Assess their posture.
- Apply controls on the same.
- Regularly monitor the posture and take action when it dips below a baseline.

3 - Introduce control mechanisms

This phase sometimes gets skipped as teams directly jump into the Zero Trust mechanism part after gathering all the data in the previous step.

You can think of this phase as a cleanup phase where you can act on all the data you have gathered. This is the part where you can:

- Conduct a risk assessment on all the data that has been gathered and remove accounts, services, and mechanisms

that are no longer needed.
- Identify those users or resources that have excessive privileges and restrict them. You can improve your security posture even before implementing anything about Zero Trust!
- Identify those services already meeting Zero Trust principles and will not require any change.
- Ensure you have a centralized directory of all user accounts with defined permissions. You can also use this phase to enforce the MFA of those accounts which might need it but still need it.

This will significantly benefit your next phase as a lot of the security baggage of previous years will have been cleaned up.

You can now use the inventory you created in the previous section to start creating high-level drafts of your Zero Trust policies and getting stakeholders' input on how they will look. Give priority to those areas which will be impacted the most, such as remote users, partners, mobile devices, etc.

Remember not to fall prey to the "shiny product" syndrome and leverage what you already have, as most controls like MFA and SSO are usually present in one form or another.

4 - Implement Zero Trust model

We finally reached the part where we can implement Zero Trust. Before reaching this phase, you should have readied the environment by removing all the unnecessary clutter from before and have policies you want to implement.

This is where you start introducing Zero Trust principles onto your existing infrastructure OR implementing those components that will enforce them. Remember to avoid making a big-bang approach but implement improvements incrementally with small wins so you can assess the impact and users can get time to understand and adapt.

You will undoubtedly encounter support and teething issues, and the policies might differ considerably from what you envisage. Try to rely on cloud-based services for your policy components instead of on-prem for longer-term scalability and remember that this roadmap has to be fluid and adaptable.

Zero Trust must be implemented phase-wise and matured over time. We will discuss Zero Trust maturity in the next section but at a high level, it can look like this.

PHASE	What happens
STARTING	<ul><li>Starting point for most companies where zero to no awareness of Zero Trust exists.</li><li>Static policies and no centralization.</li><li>Visibility into user and device posture might be</li></ul>

PHASE	What happens
	present but no decision making is done based on this contextual information. • Basic level of network segmentation may be present.
IMPROVING	• Zero Trust starts being implemented with key areas being improved in increments. • Policies start being improved to control access to data and applications. • Device and user posture starts being monitored. Cloud identity is implemented or starts implementation. • Threat Intel starts being used with minimum automation. • Microsegmentation starts
OPTIMIZED	• Companies have made large improvements in Zero Trust. • Real time analytics and threat intel is being used with cloud-based identities to control access to apps and data. • Micro segmentation has been implemented. • Network location no longer determines trust.

5 - Maintain and improve the model

A Zero Trust model must be considered a living model that evolves and improves over time. The governance committee should have periodic check-ins to see what is working and what is not. Keep going if your Zero Trust implementation differs significantly from your vision, and slowly improve it over time.

One of the best ways to improve the model is to utilize a Zero Trust maturity model that can be used as a benchmark to see where you are and where you must reach. This is an excellent way of assessing your implementation and identifying future milestones.

Numerous Zero Trust maturity models are present, but one of the best is from the Department of Homeland Security (DHS) Cybersecurity and Infrastructure Security Agency (CISA). This agency serves as the cyber risk advisor for .gov, and they break down Zero Trust implementation across five pillars:

1. **Identity**
2. **Device**
3. **Network**
4. **Application workload**
5. **Data**

The document acknowledges that zero trust takes effort to mature, so it recommends that organizations make minor improvements across these five pillars.

Each pillar can reach the following levels of maturity, which are similar to the phases we discussed earlier:

1. **Traditional zero-trust architecture**: Decisions and controls

are still primarily manual as this is the starting point. Enforcement is minimal. This is where most companies will be starting from.
2. **Initial:** Automation starts being used within policy decisions, and the groundwork is laid for advanced zero-trust decision-making.
3. **Advanced zero-trust architecture**: Automation is the name of the game here, as systems will be making most of the decisions along with continuous monitoring.
4. **Optimal zero-trust architecture:** Full automation is used along with dynamic policies. Continuous monitoring and visibility are present with contextual awareness.

The starting point for each company might differ depending on their security and technology maturity. Still, this model presents an excellent way to track where your standard in your Zero Trust journey and where you must go.

Chapter Summary

In this chapter, we saw how to start a Zero Trust journey from scratch for a company and the key steps to follow. Remember, this can be a multi-year and multi-domain project, so spread out your wins to show progress to management. We also saw how maturity models are a great way to benchmark your progress against an objective criterion. These can gauge your progress and how far you still must go.

8 – Zero Trust Challenges

We could implement Zero Trust in a perfect world and be free of all cyber threats. Unfortunately, we do not live in this world, and Zero Trust projects themselves can be subject to certain risks and challenges that we must be aware of.

Challenges to implementing ZTA.

Let us start with your challenges when implementing a Zero Trust Architecture in your company.

ZTA is a massive shift from traditional architecture and needs to be slowly phased in over some time. It can take time for the Security and Technology teams to get to grips with the same, leading to specific challenges:

- Implementation of Zero Trust might require a significant investment of time and money from the technology and IT teams. This needs to be understood and owned right from

the onset. CISOs need to communicate the value and benefit of Zero Trust to senior management and get their buy-in.
- Zero Trust Architecture might require the replacement of existing components and the implementation of entirely new ones, which can be a huge challenge. For example, Security administrators might balk at the complexity of implementing the new context-based security policies, which are the heart of the Zero Trust engine.
- The initial period might be fraught with disruptions to user access as the policies are fine-tuned and brought to an acceptable level. Extensive planning and testing can mitigate this to a degree but be prepared for new and frustrating problems to crop up!
- A critical starting point for implementing Zero Trust is to acquire a detailed inventory of all the assets present in the company, which might need to be more readily available and cause delays. Factor this into your project planning.
- Legacy applications or protocols might not support Zero Trust principles and policies.

When planning your Zero Trust journey, consider all these challenges at the start.

Lack of Zero Trust support

We saw in our earlier scenario that specific network components could not enforce Zero Trust principles leading to a phase-wise approach. Nine times out of ten, this is the scenario that you will face when implementing Zero Trust, and you must understand how to deal with it.

In this hybrid environment, you will have specific components compliant with Zero Trust principles, while others cannot enforce them. This can be an out-of-date appliance or a legacy system that does not support dynamic policies, use insecure protocols, have vulnerabilities in place that are risk accepted, and so on. Either way, it limits what integrations can be done with a Zero Trust Architecture.

Ideally, you can replace them, but sometimes these components are too critical and cannot be changed. The good news is that NIST does cater to these scenarios, and we discussed them in detail when discussing variations.

Enclave-Based deployment model

We discussed this model earlier, in which a gateway protects a collection of resources. This allows the deployment of a semi-trusted Zero Trust architecture, as you can access the resources within the enclave once authorized.

This model can be used for scenarios where legacy applications lack support for Zero Trust.

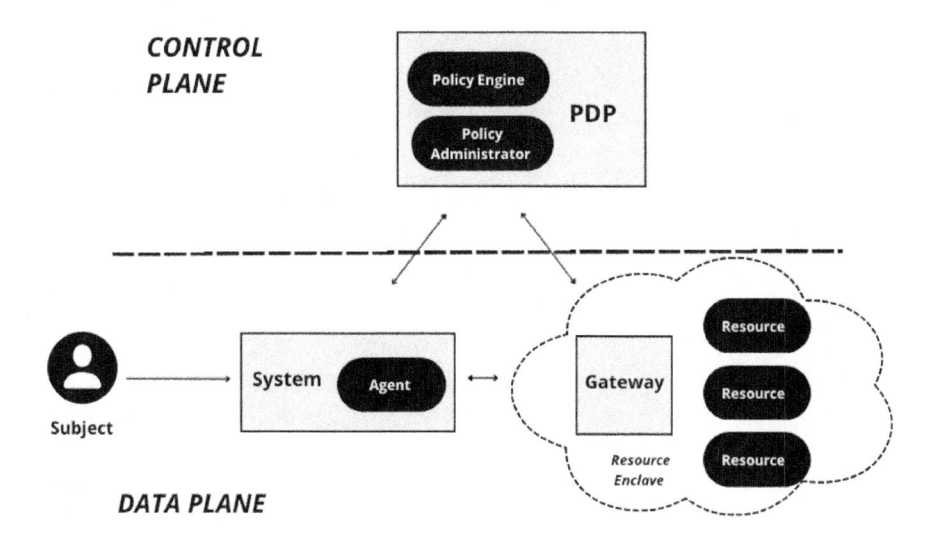

Zero Trust proxy

A practical implementation of this model is via a Zero Trust proxy. Like a traditional proxy, a Zero Trust proxy mediates connections between subjects and resources. The proxy enforces Zero Trust policies on behalf of these resources.

The Zero Trust proxy will have two components:

- The Proxy server acts as a PEP and communicates with the PDP to enforce policy decisions.
- The Proxy connector: The Proxy Server communicates with this connector once it receives permission to allow access from the Zero Trust engine. It forwards traffic to the connector, forming a secure channel between the user and

the resource.

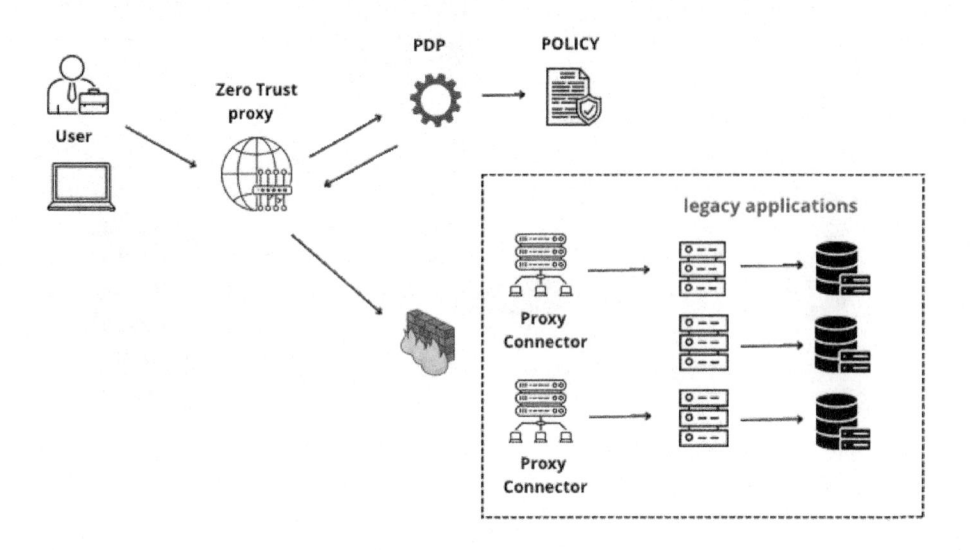

![Diagram showing User connecting through Zero Trust proxy to PDP/Policy and through Proxy Connectors to legacy applications]

This way, a secure communication channel is enforced between resources that cannot support Zero Trust. The proxy handles the heavy lifting, so the legacy resources do not have to.

A Zero Trust proxy can be a great way to implement some measure of Zero Trust where it is not supported; however, it is crucial to keep the following in mind:

- There should be no way to bypass the proxy and access the legacy applications directly. Often there are numerous inventive ways of accessing these applications via insecure protocols and other methods. This would defeat the entire zero proxy concept, so contact your admin teams to verify firewall rules and enforce new ones to limit access.
- Zero Trust proxies can be performance intensive and lack

support for all protocols. Please review the product specifications yourself and what protocols it supports before deciding. Beware of vendors promising support for every application protocol under the sun!

Chapter Summary

In this chapter, we reviewed the challenges you will almost definitely face when you start your Zero Trust journey. We also looked at the concept of a Zero Trust proxy that can help you with environments that do not support Zero Trust principles.

9 – Where to go from here

Congratulations on reaching the end of this book, and hopefully, now you understand how to implement Zero Trust practically and securely. ZTA is a technology and product agnostic and has the potential to revamp your current security model completely. It can also adapt and absorb new technologies like AI, changing the cybersecurity landscape.

My final tips for you would be:

- Refrain from falling for the hype around products that claim to implement Zero Trust but use what you already have and START.
- No single tool will implement Zero Trust. Instead, it will be a combination of solutions and processes.
- Treat it like a project rather than a solution you implement and forget about.
- Engage with key stakeholders and form a committee to track the model's performance over time.
- Each company might adopt Zero Trust differently. No "one size fits all" solution exists for a Zero Trust architecture.

Keep in touch.

I hope you enjoyed this book. Here are some of the ways you can keep in touch with me.

1. Follow me on Medium and YouTube, where I regularly discuss topics revolving around Cloud Security, AI, and Cybersecurity.

2. Check out my other book on "AI Governance and Cybersecurity" on Amazon, in which I review AI systems and how to secure them.

3. Feel free to contact me on LinkedIn if you like this book and want to discuss something. Always happy to hear from my readers!

4. Ping me at taimur74@yahoo.com if you want to contact me for any opportunities.

Training and Courses

A great way to supplement this book is to enroll in my course below, which I regularly update:

https://www.udemy.com/course/zero-trust-masterclass-from-beginner-to-mastery/

Feedback time

Thank you for reading this book, and I hope you liked it.

I would appreciate you leaving me a quick review on Amazon, and feedback will help me to improve this book further and grow as a writer. It only takes a few minutes, and I would be highly grateful.

I wish you all the best in your Zero Trust journey!

ABOUT THE AUTHOR

Taimur Ijlal is a multi-award-winning information security leader with over two decades of international experience in cyber-security and IT risk management in the fin-tech industry. He won a few awards for his contributions to the industry, including CISO of the Year, CISO Top 30, CISO Top 50, and Most Outstanding Security Team.

He served as the Head of Information Security for several major companies, but his real passion is teaching and writing about cyber-security topics. He lives in the UK where he moved with his family in 2021.

Taimur writes on Medium and has a YouTube channel, "Cloud Security Guy," on which he regularly posts about Cloud Security, Artificial Intelligence, and general cyber-security career advice. He has also launched several Cyber-Security and Artificial Intelligence courses and can be contacted on his LinkedIn profile for any consulting opportunities.

Printed in Great Britain
by Amazon